DAN MAGILL'S
Bull-Doggerel

Fifty Years of
Anecdotes from the Greatest
Bulldog Ever

LONGSTREET PRESS
Atlanta, Georgia

Published by LONGSTREET PRESS, INC.,
a subsidiary of Cox Newspapers,
a division of Cox Enterprises, Inc.
2140 Newmarket Parkway
Suite 118
Marietta, Georgia 30067

Printed in the United States of America

1st printing, 1993

Library of Congress Catalog Number 93-79659

ISBN: 1-56352-089-3

This book was printed by R. R. Donnelley & Sons, Harrisonburg, Virginia.

Jacket and book design by Jill Dible

To all Georgia Bulldogs,
whose blood runs Red and Black, from the
mountains of Hiawassee to the flatlands of Hahira,
and westward from Ludowici to Tallapoosa

To Sandy Williams,
distinguished son of my lifelong
friend Claude Williams. Even
though your education & career
have taken you to Princeton, Duke,
Harvard and Texas, I know that
in your heart you will always
be a Georgia Bulldog. Best
wishes to you and Jennifer.

Dan Magill
December '93

FOREWORD

I can still hear the music of the crack band of mighty Yale, the scourge of the East, when the team came to Athens for the dedicatory game of Sanford Stadium in 1929. As they marched from the train station up College Avenue to the Georgian Hotel, captivating the cheering crowd when they burst into "Dixie," it was then that I (eight years old, all suited out in my football uniform, ready to play) began my love affair with the University of Georgia, one which has not waned in 65 years.

Since that day it has been my good fortune to share in Georgia's glorious triumphs on the athletic fields and to know the truly great men associated with Georgia sports for a century: all nine of the university's presidents during my lifetime, from Uncle Dave Barrow up to the present chieftain Chuck Knapp; every coach of note in all sports, starting with the distinguished chemist who began football in Athens, Dr. Charles Herty; and almost every all-star athlete, beginning with Dr. John Morris, star catcher on the 1886 baseball team.

From being a "flunky" for President S. V. Sanford (on football trips to New York City), to walking home up Lumpkin Street with Athletic Director Herman Stegeman after watching football practice on old Sanford Field; from being ball-chaser and bat boy for the baseball teams of the early 1930s coached by Bill White and "Catfish" Smith, to rolling the red clay tennis courts by old Woodrulff Hall, and later to writing sports for the *Athens Banner-Herald* and the *Atlanta Journal*; I have survived to serve as UGA's sports information director for 27 years, tennis coach for 34 years, and founder and executive secretary of the Georgia Bulldog Clubs for nearly 30 years, in which capacity I had the rare pleasure of visiting members of the Great Majority Party in all 159 counties of the state. I'm also proud to have founded, in 1950, *The Georgia Bulldog* newspaper, still the voice of the Bulldogs.

But by far my greatest reward has been my association with countless other loyal Bulldogs, who are the very core of the university, the heart of its athletic program, and the inspiration for this book.

— DAN MAGILL

CONTENTS

Chapter One

ATHLETES FROM THE EARLY YEARS

1886 - 1938

THE MORRIS BROTHERS

The first intercollegiate sport at Georgia was baseball, and the captain of the first team in 1886 was an outstanding pitcher, Charles Ed Morris, who introduced the curve ball to this section of Dixie.

Charles Ed was one of three brothers famous in University of Georgia history. His younger brother John for years was head of the university's German Department, and his older brother Sylvanus was dean of the law school. Their father, Dr. Charles Morris, was a distinguished professor of Greek and Latin at Georgia, having joined the faculty shortly after the War Between the States, in which he fought as a major in the Confederate Army. Previously he had taught at William and Mary and Randolph Macon College. His father was the renowned Richard Morris, a member of the Virginia House of Burgesses, whose family had come from Wales to settle in Virginia as far back as 1732, the year George Washington was born.

Charles Ed Morris did not remain in Athens after graduation. He went up to New York City, joined an accounting firm and became quite wealthy off the stock market. But oldtimers still tell a story about Charles Ed and his brother John, who was Charles Ed's catcher on the baseball team in '86. It seems that John signaled for a curve ball, but Charles Ed cut loose with a blazing fast-ball instead! The result was a broken finger for John. And, according to the myth, the brothers did not speak to each other for many years.

I used to have a lot of fun when traveling the state speaking to Georgia Bulldog Clubs bragging that my association with Bulldog athletics went all the way back to our first team in 1886, which was true. Prof. John Morris, when he was well over 70

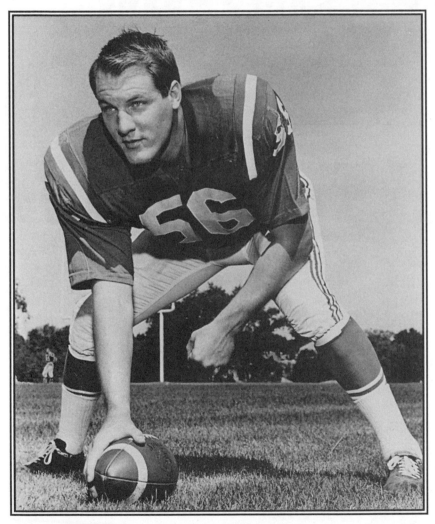

All-pro center Jon Morris, grandson of Professor John Morris

years old, taught me German. And, boy, was he a stern disciplinarian! I never saw him play baseball, but he must have had a great arm. When his students didn't pay attention, he would throw his blackboard eraser at them; and he was deadly accurate. In fact, he hit me smack in the head one time. Not because I was not paying attention—I was much too afraid of him to get out of line. Actually he was aiming at the boy sitting in front of me who ducked.

At the turn of the century Prof. John Morris was one of Georgia's first faculty chairmen of athletics. In fact, in the famous free-for-all fight that erupted during the 1912 Georgia-Alabama football game in Columbus—the result of a trick play Georgia successfully employed—Dr. Morris is remembered for a battle of fisticuffs he had with the Alabama athletic director.

Prof. Morris had a grandson, Jon Morris, who starred in football at Holy Cross and later made all-pro at center for the New England Patriots. His father, Jack Morris, wrote for the *New York Times* and at one time was head of the *Times'* Washington bureau.

Prof. John Morris' brother, Sylvanus Morris (dean of the law school), was an even more famous character on the campus— the most famous, according to dean of men William (Wild Bill) Tate, himself quite a legend. Dean Tate, on Bulldog Club trips around the state, used to regale me with tall tales, many of them about Sylvanus Morris, who lived next door to Dean Tate on historic Dearing Street in Athens.

It seems there were many things Sylvanus did not like. He especially hated automobiles and even disliked the people who drove automobiles. But, according to Dean Tate, Sylvanus never turned down an invitation to ride to church in Dean Tate's car or to return with him.

One time Sylvanus was almost run over by an automobile in front of the arch on Broad Street. He had stepped into the street, and a speeding auto would have hit him had he not quickly jumped backwards to the sidewalk, following which a companion heard him curse and mutter: "There are only two kinds of people in Athens: The QUICK and the DEAD."

Sylvanus also violently opposed the admission of women to the University. He didn't want them even to set foot on the campus or to audit classes. He had observed some of the women admitted to summer school classes—high school teachers—and he dismissed them with the comment: "These women come up here with one shirt waist and a five dollar bill and never change either one."

HAROLD "WAR EAGLE" KETRON

In 1946 Georgia's squad was loaded with boys from Pennsylvania, headed by All-Americans Charley Trippi of Pittston and Johnny Rauch of Yeadon. Coach Butts scheduled the Temple game in Philadelphia so the families of our Pennsylvania boys could see them play—the original reason the Temple games were scheduled.

There used to be a joke back then that Georgia had more Pennsylvanians than Fred Waring did, whose famous band was known as The Pennsylvanians.

The man responsible for Georgia's recruiting Pennsylvanians was Harold (War Eagle) Ketron, head of the Coca-Cola Company in Eastern Pennsylvania. Mr. Ketron acquired his nickname as a boy playing cow-pasture football in the hills of Habersham County, Georgia. He was a rough and tumble player and received so many cuts and bruises that his father, a mountain doctor who lived in Clarkesville, spent a lot of time sewing up his own son. Dr. Ketron frowned on football because he thought boys ought to do more than engage in brawls while chasing an oblong ball, and he was happy when his son headed for the state university in Athens to get some learning and polishing. But only a few weeks later Dr. Ketron was horrified to read in the *Atlanta Constitution* that a Georgia football game had ended in a free-for-all-fight and that one of the combatants was a Harold Ketron of Clarkesville, Georgia. Dr. Ketron promptly dispatched a letter to his son, ordering him to withdraw from school and return home to the farm.

When young Ketron showed this letter to his coach, Billy Reynolds, the coach and star player immediately set out for Clarkesville to see Dr. Ketron. Coach Reynolds did a masterful job of explaining to Dr. Ketron that football had more virtues than sins, and Dr. Ketron decided to let his son remain in school.

But War Eagle was not through with his fighting days by a long shot. In 1903 against Vanderbilt, as captain of the Georgia team, he objected to Vanderbilt Coach Henry's yelling instructions to his players on the field, a practice which was against the rules in those days. When the officials wouldn't do anything about it, Captain Ketron took matters into his own hands. He

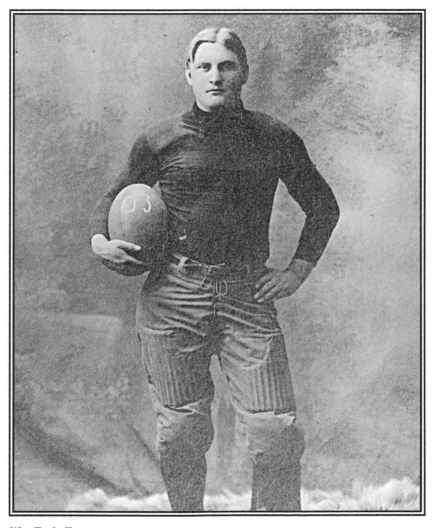

War Eagle Ketron

went over and knocked Coach Henry down.

Another story on War Eagle also occurred in 1903. When Clemson, under young Coach John Heisman, was winning the Southern championship, the Tigers beat Georgia 29-0. After the game War Eagle told the Clemson players—scheduled to play Georgia Tech next—that he would give them a bushel of apples for each point Clemson beat Tech worse than Clemson had beaten Georgia. Clemson whipped Tech to the tune of 73-0. War Eagle had to pick 44 bushels of apples off his dad's orchard near Clarkesville.

After World War I, War Eagle had a job in the United States House of Representatives as Sergeant of Arms, and he acquired quite a reputation for being able to quell disturbances on the floor. He always quickly restored order in the House.

When Mr. Ketron became head of the Coca-Cola Company in Eastern Pennsylvania, with headquarters in Wilkes-Barre, he still loved football and would referee high school games as a hobby. He saw many good football players whom he would later recommend to Georgia. He'd also give them summer jobs driving Coca-Cola trucks around the Wilkes-Barre area.

War Eagle Ketron was Georgia's secret weapon during Coach Butts' glory days at Georgia in the 1940s.

MORTON HODGSON, ONE OF GEORGIA'S MOST VERSATILE ATHLETES EVER

Georgia's baseball team of 1908 for many years was the most revered of all Bulldog athletic teams, football included. It won the old Southern Intercollegiate Conference, winning 20 straight games en route to the crown, and 11 of them were shutouts (six in succession). Actually, it was not until the 1927 football Bulldogs won nine straight games (and ranked no. 1 in the country until they lost their finale to Georgia Tech) that a football team was more popular with old-time Georgia fans than the celebrated 1908 baseball juggernaut. Originally, baseball was the premier college sport; football didn't really overtake it until well after World War I.

The 1908 diamond 'Dogs had many stars, including Georgia's first player to make the big leagues in professional ball: second baseman Claude Derrick of Clayton who later played with Connie Mack's world champion Philadelphia Athletics.

Another standout was its heavy-hitting first baseman, Morton Hodgson, a hometown boy whom Grantland Rice named to his All-Southern team. Hodgson was a four-letter athlete and for

Morton Hodgson, Sr., (right) with John Carson

years was considered Georgia's most versatile athlete ever.

He played the four major sports in college (football, halfback and end; basketball, forward; track, hurdles; baseball, first base and pitcher). After college he remained active as an outstanding local golfer and tennis player, having a nice clay court in his side yard on Prince Avenue in Athens where he invited me to play several times when I was a boy.

As an indication of what a wonderful athlete Morton Hodgson must have been, one should consider the fact that in 1955 at the age of 65 (just six months before he died of a heart attack), he shot one-under par 35 for nine holes in a special exhibition against a modern Georgia four-letter athlete, Long John Carson, at the Athens Country Club. Carson was an All-American in golf and football, and he also shot a 35 that day.

Morton had three sons who were good athletes, too. Morton Jr. captained the Georgia swimming team and later headed the Coca-Cola operations in South America. Middle son Hutch lettered at guard under Harry Mehre in 1933, and youngest son, Robert, was a brilliant all-round high school athlete who died during World War II as an army pilot.

Morton also is the only Georgia athlete who has had two grandsons to play football at Georgia: Pat Hodgson (son of Hutch), all-SEC end in 1965, and Josh Watt (son of daughter Nell), tight end in 1975.

Incidentally, when Morton's daughter Nell was married to Bob Watt they had the biggest wedding party ever held in Athens. The stars of Coca-Cola's national radio show (Irish tenor Morton Downey, comedian Edgar Bergen and Charley McCarthy) came down to Athens and regaled the wedding guests. How did that come about? Well, Nell's aunt, the first Nell Hodgson (Morton's sister and for whom young Nell was named) was the wife of the man known as "Mr. Anonymous," Bob Woodruff, head of Coca-Cola.

The Hodgsons have long been a distinguished family in Athens, the first member, Edward Hodgson, arriving in 1839 from England where he was a carriage maker. Many of his numerous descendants have been prominent in University of Georgia circles. One of them, Hugh Hodgson, for years was head of the University's music department and was famous throughout the state for his Georgia Glee Club tours. In fact, Hugh and his equally illustrious cousin, Morton, collaborated on a Georgia fight song that is still played by the Redcoat band: "Going Back to Old Athens Town."

THE IMMORTAL BOB MCWHORTER

When I used to travel the state to Georgia Bulldog Club meetings, frequently I would be asked the question, "You've been around Georgia so long, did you know Bob McWhorter?" To which I would reply, "Did I know Bob McWhorter! Why, I'll have you know that I played in the same backfield with Bob McWhorter," which was no lie. I did play in the same backfield with Bob McWhorter, Jr. (Marse Bob's son), in intramural football at Georgia just prior to World War II.

I never had the pleasure of seeing Bob McWhorter play football (his last game for Georgia in 1913 was eight years before I was born), but I did know Mr. Bob and many members of the large and distinguished McWhorter clan. The original McWhorters, by the way, came to Delaware from Ireland, in the early days of this country, then migrated on down to Virginia and North Carolina and eventually to Georgia.

Both Bob's father and grandfather (the original Robert Ligon McWhorter for whom Bob was named) graduated at Georgia.

Bob was born in Lexington, only 15 miles from Athens, on June 4, 1891, but his boyhood home was the McWhorter plantation "big house" located on the highest ground of what is now Cloverhurst avenue in Athens, which was just three short blocks from my boyhood home on Cherokee Avenue. And, my present home on Woodlawn was built on land where Judge Hamilton McWhorter (Bob's father) planted cotton for many years, the same cotton fields where young Bob played as a boy and was so fast (according to his younger brother Howard) that he could run down rabbits.

All five of Judge McWhorter's sons were good athletes at Georgia: Marcus, Hamilton Jr. and Howard excelled in baseball; Bob and Thurmond (the youngest) in football. Bob also starred

Bob McWhorter, Georgia's first All-American

in baseball, being considered the South's best player (heavy-hitting center fielder), and it was believed he could have been an outstanding professional player like his contemporary and fellow north Georgian, Ty Cobb of nearby Royston. But Bob chose a career in law instead.

However, I did see Bob McWhorter play baseball. That is, I saw him play "softball" on old Herty Field in the late 1930s when Mr.

Bob was in his late 40s. It was a game between the UGA faculty all-stars (Mr. Bob taught law) and the fraternity league intramural all-stars, and Bob McWhorter hit the longest softball home run I have ever seen. Home plate was in front of the chapel bell, and Mr. Bob smacked the ball over the center fielder's head past the old Beanery (now the School of Landscape Architecture and Environmental Design) and all the way to Lumpkin street.

Yes, I certainly did know Bob McWhorter, but not as well as my father (editor of the *Athens Banner-Herald*), who was one of his closest friends and was instrumental in getting Mr. Bob to run for mayor, an office he held for many years. And it was by far the biggest honor of my life to represent my deceased father as a pall bearer at Mr. Bob's funeral at the First Baptist Church in June of 1960.

Bob McWhorter was unarguably Georgia's greatest football player during our first half-century of football. He was named All-Southern from 1910 through 1913, and during an era when it was almost impossible for a Southerner to make the Yankee sportswriters' All-America teams, he became Georgia's first All-American in 1913.

The man who knew Bob McWhorter's football accomplishments best, his "Boswell," was the late Charlie Martin, who was in school at Georgia throughout McWhorter's brilliant career. And, Charlie, who was an Athens sportswriter and newspaperman before becoming Georgia's business manager of athletics in the 1920s and early 1930s, many times regaled me with his hero's exploits. Some of the highlights I well remember:

■ Bob McWhorter's first official athletic competition was at Gordon Military College in Barnesville, where he played under Coach Alex Cunningham. Their baseball team came up to Athens one spring and beat Georgia, 11-0. Dr. S. V. Sanford, Georgia's faculty chairman of athletics, that same day hired Cunningham to be Georgia's football and baseball coach. Cunningham was a disciple of Dan McGugin who had made Vanderbilt the football power in the South, and McGugin was a disciple of Fielding Yost who had made Michigan the mightiest team in the land. Cunningham brought McWhorter to Georgia with him in the fall of 1910 as a freshman although Bob was just a junior at Gordon. Dr. Sanford wanted Bob at Georgia, so it was "arranged."

■ Bob McWhorter led Georgia to victory over Georgia Tech his freshman year on the strength of a 45-yard run late in the game, which ended a five-year winning streak by the John Heisman-coached Yellow Jackets. This feat made McWhorter an instant Bulldog hero, and he went on to lead Georgia to three more wins over Georgia Tech, an even more remarkable feat when it is realized that all games were played on The Enemy's home field in Atlanta. Once McWhorter graduated, Tech and Heisman resumed their winning ways over Georgia.

■ In 1913 in Atlanta, Tech dedicated its new stadium, Grant Field, by playing Georgia with a record crowd of 10,000 on hand. Heisman had devised a defense that he thought could stop McWhorter. His linemen slanted on their charges into the Bulldog backfield toward McWhorter, and they did bottle him up most of the game. But Coach Cunningham countered by feeding the ball to another Bulldog back, Stephen Crump, who had a field day. Georgia won, 14-0, with none other than Bob McWhorter scoring the final TD on a one-yard plunge. Tech students, by the way, were so confident that they would upset Georgia that they pledged not to shave until Christmas if they lost (the game was played November 15, almost six weeks before Christmas!).

■ McWhorter graduated from Georgia with an A.B. degree in 1914, Phi Beta Kappa, Phi Kappa Phi, and was elected to Sphinx as a junior. He received his law degree from Virginia in 1917, and while he was at Virginia, the Cavaliers went up to Boston to play perennial national champion Harvard. There the Boston sportswriters wrote that Virginia had a mysterious halfback by the name of "Bob White," who was the best runner they had ever seen. It is said that "Bob White" was really Bob McWhorter, but Mr. Bob never admitted it to me. He always merely smiled when I asked him about this story. But it is well known that in the old days schools often played "ringers."

■ McWhorter's main asset as a football player was his ball-carrying ability, but he was a good all-round player, excelling on defense and also as a blocker and passer. He was powerfully built (about 5-10, 185 pounds with a lot of strength in his legs and hips—like Frank Sinkwich) and he had very good speed. Georgia didn't pass much, but McWhorter won several games with his passing. In his day a player could pass out of bounds in lieu of punting, and Bob had the strongest arm of any player in Dixie. His most famous pass beat Auburn on Thanksgiving Day in Athens in 1912. It was fourth down, the score tied 6-6 late in the game, when McWhorter went back to pass out of bounds instead of punting, but the ball slipped in his hand and didn't go out of bounds. Instead, a surprised end, Hugh Conklin, caught it in the end zone for the winning score. Bob liked to tell this story about his greatest pass.

Bob McWhorter scored 61 touchdowns during his four seasons at Georgia. The school record is listed as 52 by one Herschel Walker, and it should be corrected. Bob McWhorter was Georgia's first inductee into the National Football Foundation's Hall of Fame, and it is most appropriate that the Bulldogs' athletic dormitory is named for this modest and most gifted athlete, Athens' most revered son.

———— ■ ————

No less than nine members of the distinguished McWhorter family have starred on athletic teams at the University of Georgia during the 20th century, and several more have been closely associated with Bulldog teams in various capacities. Currently, Georgia assistant football coach Hamilton Pierce (Mac) McWhorter, an all-SEC offensive guard in 1973, is carrying on this grand tradition.

Mac's father, Pierce, was an outstanding high school athlete at old Atlanta Tech High (fullback in football and catcher in baseball), but he is one of the few McWhorters not to matriculate at Georgia. Actually, he signed a Georgia football grant-in-aid in 1947 but changed his mind in order to play professional baseball with the old Atlanta Crackers. Baseball was in his blood. His father (Coach Mac's grandfather), the late Marcus McWhorter, was a legendary Georgia baseball player in the early 1900s, compiling a career batting average of .460.

Marcus was the oldest of Judge Hamilton McWhorter's five sons; his younger brother Hamilton pitched a no-hit game vs. Vanderbilt; Hamilton had a son, Jim (Red) McWhorter, who was a first-string blocking back for Coach Frank Thomas at Alabama and who was a classmate of mine at old Athens High. We were on the tennis team together and won the 10th district high school doubles in 1938.

The best player of the group, according to Howard McWhorter, was the oldest brother, Marcus, although Bob (Georgia's first All-America football player and the most famous of them all) received professional baseball offers and turned them down to pursue a law career.

There is a good story about a bunt Marcus once made. His Georgia coach was an Irishman by the name of Tommy Stouch, who sent Marcus to bat with instructions to bunt, but Marcus didn't know how to bunt. He hit the first pitch for a home run out of the park at old Herty Field. Whereupon Coach Stouch ran up to Marcus as he crossed home plate and said to him in his Irish brogue loud enough for all the fans to hear, "Faith and me Christ, I've been in professional baseball 20 years and that is the longest bunt me eyes have ever seen."

The first McWhorter on Georgia's athletic scene was Robert Boyd McWhorter of Woodville in Greene County. He was manager of the 1899 football team. His first cousins, brothers Vason McWhorter Jr. and Fonville McWhorter of Woodville, played on the Georgia team a few years later.

Following in the footsteps of Bob McWhorter, who played halfback from 1910 through 1913, was his youngest brother, Thurmond, who played halfback in 1919-20.

Vason McWhorter III of Woodville, whose father had played in 1903, captained Georgia's 1932 team and was a fine center.

Bill McWhorter of Buckhead in Morgan county, played halfback in 1965-66 and was instrumental in a great victory over Alabama in 1965.

To take a broader view of the McWhorter lineage, the first McWhorter to set foot in Georgia was Hugh McWhorter who moved to Georgia in 1803 and settled at Potts Branch, Oglethorpe county. He married Helen Ligon of Virginia in 1810. She was a descendent of Thomas Ligon, a member of the Virginia House of Burgesses in 1655.

This Hugh McWhorter was a descendent of another Hugh McWhorter, a linen merchant of County Armagh, Ireland, who came to America and settled in Newcastle, Delaware. His family had moved to Ireland from Scotland, where the McWhorters were a part of the Buchanan clan, which produced the fifteenth president of the United States, James Buchanan.

Dr. Boyd McWhorter, Georgia's faculty chairman of athletics from 1965 until 1972 when he became commissioner of the Southeastern Conference, also is a descendent of Hugh McWhorter of Potts Branch, Oglethorpe County.

Commissioner McWhorter's father was Hezzie McWhorter of Cochran, who was a member of the Georgia State House of Representatives from Bleckley County. Hezzie's brother was State Senator Hamilton McWhorter of Oglethorpe County, whose son "Hamp" McWhorter, Jr., was the long time secretary of the Georgia State Senate and a former Georgia basketball manager. Hamilton McWhorter, Sr., also was the grandfather of Hamilton Jordan of Albany, chief of staff for President Jimmy Carter.

There is a good story about the brothers Hezzie and Hamilton when they were legislators at the state capital together. Hezzie wanted brother Hamilton, who was president of the State Senate, to help him get a particular bill passed through the senate. When he asked brother Hamilton for his aid, Hamilton replied:

"I'll do the best I can, Hezzie," to which Hezzie retorted: "Hell, if that's all you can do, just forget about it."

DEAN WILLIAM (WILD BILL) TATE

One of the handsomest buildings on the Georgia campus is the Student Center, and it couldn't have been named for anyone who better served his alma mater than he: Dean William Tate.

To the alumni of the past half century Dean Tate undoubtedly is the best remembered Georgia faculty-staff member. However, not many know that this Georgia mountaineer was one of Georgia's all-time great athletes. In his prime, during the 1920s, he was the South's premier distance runner.

In the 1930s Dean Tate was the assistant dean of men to the famous Herman Stegeman, who had retired as Georgia's athletic director. "Stege," who had been Dean Tate's track coach, loved to tell this story on how Dean Tate got the best of him one time.

Dean William Tate

Dean Tate had been quite an idol for the young track men in the state, one of whom was a Macon lad by the name of Bob Young (later to be conference champion at Georgia). Young wrote his hero in Athens for advice on how to run the mile, and Dean Tate gladly sent him postcard instructions each week. That summer, to the surprise of the Georgia star, the high school boy showed up at Birmingham for the Southern AAU mile race. The teacher and his pupil ran neck and neck for three laps, but coming down the stretch the high school boy put on a burst of speed and beat his teacher to the tape.

Whereupon, Coach Stegeman ran up to his star miler, Tate, and exclaimed, "What happened? How could you lose to this high school boy?"

To which the star miler replied: "Well, I guess he just had a smarter coach than I did."

There are numerous remarkable stories on Dean Tate almost right up to the day he died. He rallied from a coma to dictate his last column for an Athens newspaper. Unusual? Not for Dean Tate. His column was due and as long as there was breath in his body, Dean Tate would fulfill his obligations.

Although Dean Tate's accomplishments at Georgia are well known by alumni, I think the best thing he ever did was to marry Sue Fan Barrow. Granddaughter of the university's beloved Chancellor Dave Barrow, reared on the campus and steeped in all its traditions, Sue Fan was the perfect choice to be his wife. And those of us who have known her warmth and graciousness, her intelligence and gentleness recognize her as being the central force in his life.

Dean Tate was rightfully proud of his family. I remember when his son Ben was just a toddler, Dean Tate liked to walk him on Monday evenings from his home on Dearing Street to visit various sorority and fraternity houses on Milledge Avenue, where Ben would lisp, "To hell with Tech," at the nudging of his beaming father.

Some years ago I was awakened in the early morning hours by a phone call from a nearby town. One of my tennis players had experienced an encounter with "the law." Cursing, I got dressed and drove through the darkness to the nearby town. When I arrived, I was met not only by the tennis player but also by Dean Tate. He was there to offer support and the vast resources of the university—if needed—to that student. No matter what punishment Dean Tate would rightfully mete out later, in that moment of need, Dean Tate was there.

To me, no incident better typifies Dean Tate. And, to countless hundreds of Georgia students and also their parents, it was reassuring to know that no matter what the circumstances, in moments of need Dean Tate was there. Now the Dean Tate Center is there for thousands of Georgia students, providing countless services, the same as Dean Tate did for so long.

SPURGEON CHANDLER

Back in the spring of 1928 an Athens ice-cream salesman was driving through the red clay hills of northeast Georgia headed for Carnesville, the county seat of Franklin. He came to a fork in the dirt road and there was not a sign indicating which way to Carnesville. But he noticed a husky, freckled-face, auburn-haired boy by the side of the road plowing a cotton field. So he asked the boy for directions.

Lo and behold, the boy picked up the plow with his right arm and pointed the way to Carnesville.

This feat greatly impressed the ice-cream salesman, who also happened to be a staunch University of Georgia football supporter by the name of Larry Costa. Mr. Costa struck up a conversation with the boy and learned that he had played football, baseball and track (threw the javelin) at Franklin County high school and had been offered a football scholarship to Clemson but would prefer to go to his native state university in Athens.

When Mr. Costa returned to Athens he reported the incident to Georgia's head football coach, Harry Mehre, who followed up and informed the boy that he would give him a scholarship if he made the team. The boy came to Athens, and he made the team.

Ole Timer, the *Atlanta Journal's* famous sportswriter whose real name was Edwin Camp (a Georgia alumnus), later heard Mr. Costa's story through Coach Mehre, and Ole Timer immortalized this Georgia country boy as "The Carnesville Plowboy." His name was and is Spurgeon Chandler.

Coach Mehre recalls Chandler as a great athlete but even a greater competitor: a very conscientious player who blamed himself, never others, whenever he did not do as well as he wanted. Chandler had a burning desire to win, the same quality possessed to such a high degree by his fellow Franklin Countian and fellow red-head, the Georgia Peach himself, Ty Cobb.

Spurgeon Chandler

Coach Mehre also recalls that Chandler almost failed his major course at Georgia, which was plowing (he was in the ag school). Actually, Chandler was a fine plower, but on one big test the professor discovered that Chandler had left almost half an acre unplowed because he had cut the corners.

Chandler had an outstanding athletic career in both football and baseball. He was a genuine triple-threat left halfback in the

Notre Dame box formation and a first-stringer for three years of winning football with the Bulldogs in 1929-30-31. He was one of the Flaming Sophomores of 1929 who blanked Yale, 15-0, in the dedicatory game of Sanford Stadium. He threw a touchdown pass to All-American end, Vernon (Catfish) Smith. Chandler was a fine punter, too, and also a first-class defensive back.

Coach Mehre recalls another story about Chandler when he signed a bonus contract with the New York Yankees after his final baseball season at Georgia in May 1932. Mehre says Chandler spent most of his bonus riding in a Yellow Cab to his classes on Ag Hill.

Chandler pitched 10 years with the New York Yankees although often handicapped by injuries. An arm injury finally forced his retirement in 1947, but he had won 109 games and lost only 43 for a 71.7 winning percentage, still the best in major league history for a career covering 10 years or more.

In 1943 Chandler was acclaimed the best pitcher in baseball. He compiled a 20-4 record in pitching the Yankees to the American League pennant, and his earned run average of 1.64 was the best in the American League since Walter Johnson in his heyday. He also won two games in leading the Yankees to another World Series championship, and he won baseball's coveted Most Valuable Player Award.

After Army service in 1944 and 1945, Chandler returned to the Yankees for one more great season in 1946. He won 20 and lost eight. That season, the Yankees' legendary catcher, Bill Dickey, then managing the Yankees, said Chandler was the best pitcher he ever caught.

"Chandler is a master of five pitches," said Dickey: "the fastball, the curve, the slider, the forkball and the screwball. You can call for any of them at any time."

When Joe McCarthy, the Yankees' most celebrated manager, retired, he named an all-time New York Yankee team. His pitching staff of three consisted of Lefty Gomez, Red Ruffing and Spurgeon Chandler.

It was no surprise when, in 1969, the Georgia Hall of Fame added to its distinguished roll of members the name of the Carnesville Plowboy, Spurgeon Chandler.

The Catfish

With a nickname like "Catfish," you had to be something special, and Vernon "Catfish" Smith was one of the most colorful and brilliant athletes ever to wear the Red and Black.

As a boy in the middle Georgia town of Macon, he acquired his celebrated moniker by biting off the head of an Ocmulgee River catfish to win a wager from high school buddies.

A few years later he became considerably more famous when he scored all 15 points as Georgia upset mighty Yale, 15-0, in the 1929 dedicatory game of Sanford Stadium. He scored Georgia's first TD on a short pass from Spurgeon Chandler and then kicked the extra point. He also tackled Yale's All-America scatback, little Albie Booth, for a safety and recovered a blocked Yale punt in the end zone for another TD.

He went on to win All-Southern Conference honors at end three straight years: 1929-31. He was named to the All-America first team his senior season and in 1979 was inducted into the National Collegiate Hall of Fame.

Although Catfish was most famous for his football exploits, he was outstanding in basketball and baseball, too. In fact, the *Atlanta Journal*'s great writer Edwin Camp thought he was Georgia's very best athlete "in the clutch."

I have often heard Camp recall the time Catfish led Georgia to the Southern Conference basketball title in 1932 in the annual tournament at the old Atlanta Auditorium. Georgia had made it to the finals against North Carolina but would not have its star center, Bill Strickland of Buchanan, Georgia, for the big game. Strickland had sprained an ankle, so Catfish moved from forward to center and did such a fine job against the Tarheel's all-star center, Edwards, that Georgia held a 26-24 lead with only 10 seconds left in the game. It was then that Catfish intercepted a Tarheel shot for goal and started hell-bent down the floor. Knowing all was lost, two Carolinians knocked Catfish clear off the court. As he rose and started to the foul line, the pistol sounded to end the game. Catfish declined the free shots and promptly turned to shake hands with the Carolina captain.

I like to recall Catfish's final performance as a Georgia Bulldog, which was in the fourth and final game of the baseball

Vernon (Catfish) Smith

series against The Enemy on old Sanford Field. The Yellow
Jackets were coached by none other than Bobby Dodd. In the
bottom of the tenth inning, with the score tied 9-9 and Hut
Parks on second with two outs, Catfish Smith came to bat.
Already he had blasted two triples, a double and a single. Now,
on a three-two pitch, he lined a bullet deep to left field. As
Catfish reached second base, he saw Parks crossing the plate

with the winning run. Slowly and with bowed head, he faced about and walked toward the bench. As his teammates were shaking his hand, an 11-year-old boy (me) was retrieving the ball that Catfish had lined deep into the left field corner and that the Tech outfielder knew had ended the game as soon as he heard the crack of the bat.

Forty years later, in 1972, I saw Catfish for what I believe was the last time. He had come to Athens from Hawaii, where he was living at the time, to watch his daughter, Paula (who had been visiting relatives in Macon) easily win the Crackerland Tennis Championship for girls 16-and-under.

Catfish was very proud of Paula, who went on to be one of the world's finest doubles players. She won the Italian Open doubles with Candy Reynolds in 1981 and played on the victorious U.S. Wightman Cup team in 1983 with Martina Navratilova and Pam Shriver.

The Unforgettable Fred Birchmore

One of the most amazing Georgia Bulldog athletes (and individuals) without a doubt was Fred Birchmore. And I should say "still is" because at age 82 he still works all day in his yard and starts off each day (around 5:00 a.m.) jogging several miles around the UGA quarter mile track.

Fred began his athletic career at the Athens YMCA, being a protege of the Y's legendary physical director, Clarence Jones, better known as just plain "Jonesey."

Tumbling and boxing were Fred's strong points, and it's a shame Georgia didn't have a gymnastics team in Fred's day because he would have given the Bulldogs a champion gymnast. I recall him "walking on his hands" all the way down one side of Sanford Stadium (before the hedge had grown up), across the playing field and up the other side of the stadium without a stop.

Georgia did have a boxing team, though, and Fred was a star mittman, being reunited with his old mentor at the Athens Y, "Jonesey," who had taken a new job as Georgia's football trainer, boxing and swimming coach. Fred won the old Southern Conference bantam-weight title for 119-pounders in 1930.

Fred is famous for many other feats, though. Perhaps his greatest was his world bicycle trip in 1934 and 1935. He began in the summer of 1934 by touring Europe. He studied international law in Germany at Cologne from October through mid-

Fred Birchmore with "Bucephelus"

February, then began the rest of the trip. He cycled down through the Alps to Egypt, across Central Asia, then 1,300 miles down the Grand Trunk Road to Mandalay; below the Burma Road to the Malay Peninsula; through Thailand and French Indo-China (now Vietnam); caught a rice boat across the China Sea to the Philippines; worked his passage on an oriental freighter to California; then pedaled across the USA back to Athens. Just about 25,000 miles!

He named his bicycle Bucephalus for Alexander the Great's famous warhorse. Fred's "Bucephalus" long has been in the Smithsonian Institute in Washington. When I visited there in 1941 it was standing next to Lindbergh's "Spirit of St. Louis."

In 1939 Fred and an Athens friend, Willie Broach, bicycled to the World's Fair in New York in seven days, then across Canada to the World's Fair at Treasure Island, California, then down to Mexico and back to Athens—12,000 miles in four months. They averaged 100 miles per day.

Later in 1939 Fred and a Georgia co-ed, the former Wiladean Stuckey of Brunswick, were married; they spent their honeymoon on a two-seated bike, touring Latin America. They went 6,000 miles, including 600 miles through Cuba.

Fred and Wiladean had four children, all good tennis players: Becky, who became top-ranked women's player in the state, Fred Jr., Linda and Danny.

Fred named his youngest child Daniel Alexander for Daniel in the Lion's Den and Alexander the Great, and both of those great warriors would have been proud of their namesake. Danny Birchmore was a great tennis player, who won the U.S. Boys' (18 and under) clay court singles (upsetting Jimmy Connors in the quarter-finals), and he led Georgia to its first SEC team title in 1971, twice making All-America. He chose a medical career instead of pro tennis.

Fred has many hobbies. One of them is arrowhead collecting, and his collection of over 50,000 is considered one of the finest —possibly the best—private collections in the country.

Germany had its Frederick the Great. Athens has its Fred the Great.

THE INDOMITABLE FORREST (SPECK) TOWNS

It was certainly fitting that Georgia's track was named for the Bulldogs' legendary 1936 Olympic champion and longtime coach, the incomparable and indomitable Forrest Grady (Speck) Towns.

When Speck was born February 6, 1904, in Fitzgerald, Georgia, his father (a railroad man) must have known that his red-haired, freckled-faced son was destined for greatness. He named him for two illustrious Southerners: Gen. Nathan Bedford Forrest, Confederate States of America cavalry officer, and Henry W. Grady, editor and orator who led the South's resurgence after we had lost a close one against a stacked deck.

It was General Forrest who said, when asked the secret of his military success: "I believe in getting thar the fustest with the mostest."

Speck Towns also believed in getting "thar fustest" as he almost always did in his hurdle races.

Speck was the greatest champion and most defiant competitor I have ever known. How he won a track scholarship to Georgia is a story that made *Ripley's Believe-It-Or-Not.* Speck had played football at Richmond Academy in Augusta but not well enough to attract the college scouts. Following graduation he worked two years, including a stint as a taxi cab driver, and it was during this period that an Augusta sports editor, Tom Wall, while visiting a friend who lived next door to the Towns family, noticed Speck high-jumping in the Towns' backyard. Wall saw Speck place a bar on top of the heads of his father and younger brother, at a height slightly over six feet, and clear it with a running approach that resembled a horse jumping a hurdle. Actually, Speck as a boy used to walk horses in Augusta horse shows, after which he'd try to imitate their form in jumping fences and boxes. So Wall wrote in his column the next day that some college was missing a winner in the high jump by not having this young man. A Georgia alumnus clipped out this article and sent it to Georgia track coach Weems Baskin, who promptly invited Speck to Athens for a tryout.

In little over two years (28 months) after Coach Baskin, a

Forrest (Speck) Towns

champion hurdler himself at Auburn, introduced Speck to hurdling in the spring of 1934, he became the Olympic champion and world's record holder—an incredible and unparalleled achievement by both pupil and coach. And Speck held the world's record for 14 years (1936 to 1950), one of the longest spans a world mark has been held. Offhand, I can think of only one world's record that lasted a longer time. That was the 100-

meter freestyle mark in swimming set by Tarzan of the Apes, I mean Johnny Weissmuller.

Georgia's Olympic champion high hurdler didn't have to play football at Georgia. He was on a track scholarship. But he liked football and lettered as a substitute end in 1936 and 1937. He was rather thin to play end at 6-1, 155 pounds, but he enjoyed the competition so much that he played four years of football, counting his freshman season. He was a punt-covering specialist and may have been the best to ever wear the Red and Black. One year he did such an outstanding job keeping the Georgia Tech punt returners bottled up that Coach William Alexander of Tech named him to the Yellow Jackets' all-opponent team.

Speck also is listed in the Georgia football record book with a 65-yard touchdown run against LSU in Baton Rouge in 1936, just a few weeks following his Olympic victory at Berlin. He picked up a loose ball following a blocked kick and displayed Olympian speed en route to the end zone.

Incidentally, it must have been fate that gave Speck the chance to set his long-standing world's record. A few days after the Olympics he received a telegram from Georgia football coach Harry Mehre that said: "Minor sports now over. Report for football practice September 1." But the AAU refused to let Speck return home until he had run in International AAU exhibition races at Hamburg, London, Stockholm, Paris and Oslo.

It was at Oslo that he broke his own Olympic and world's record time of 14.1 seconds for the 110-meter high hurdles with an unbelievable clocking of 13.7 seconds. At Oslo the timers were amazed when they read their watches at 13.7 seconds. Towns had crossed the finish line before his closest competitor, O' Connor of Canada, had reached the final hurdle. At the 1938 I.A.A.F. meeting to hear world record claims, Great Britain recommended for approval a 14 seconds-flat performance by both O'Connor of Canada and Lavarett of South Africa. But the Norwegian delegation, pushing Towns' time of 13.7, showed movies of this much-discussed race which showed Towns finishing 15 yards in front of O' Connor. It served to get Towns' time approved as the world's record and it stood 14 years.

In his prime (mid-summer 1935 through mid-summer 1937)

Towns won over 60 consecutive races, a miraculous achievement in one of the most difficult and exacting athletic events.

——— ■ ———

When Coach Baskin gave Speck Towns a scholarship, he thought his young recruit could develop into a high jump champion. But even though Speck could clear a few inches over six feet with his natural "horse jumping" style, he never could improve by using the conventional styles of college high jumpers (the Eastern and Western rolls) that Coach Baskin taught him.

So Coach Baskin decided to try him at hurdling, and I actually saw Speck try to clear his first hurdle. It was in the spring of 1934. I was a boy of 13, grazing on the fresh bermuda grass shoots by Georgia's old track, where the Tate Center now stands. I was lying on the grass between the baseball field and the track close by the straightaway where the hurdles were run, waiting for Georgia track practice to end, at which time I would practice pole vaulting (I aspired to be a high school vaulter).

All of a sudden, I noticed a hurdler hit a hurdle and go sprawling on the cinders. He angrily got up and began cussing. I had grown up at the Athens Young Men's Christian Association (YMCA) and, at that time, had never missed a Sunday School class at the Athens First Baptist. So you can imagine what a shock it was for me listening to this would-be hurdler deliver the finest recitation of foul language my young ears had ever heard. It made a marked impression on me and I went over and asked another Georgia trackman the name of that champion cusser. He replied, "Speck Towns."

Speck became my boyhood idol. I told some of my friends about him, and we would come down and watch him run the hurdles, hoping he'd knock one over, fall down again, and give another cussing performance. Speck didn't know my name, but one day he must have noticed that I had been watching him every afternoon. He walked by where I was grazing on the grass and said: "Hi, Red." (I used to have hair back then and it happened to be red.) I started to reply, "And how are you today, Red," because his hair was redder than mine. But I just said, "Howdy, Mr. Speck." Incidentally, Speck in those days had more freckles than anybody I had ever seen except a trout I caught up in Rabun County.

———— ■ ————

Back in the late 1960s, the Augusta Georgia Bulldog Club was holding its annual meeting at the Augusta Country Club. They had invited native son Speck to be guest of honor, but he couldn't make it since he was with his Georgia trackmen at an indoor meet up East. Speck asked me to tell the club how much he appreciated the invitation, though. Well, we were celebrating another Georgia SEC football championship that night, and I plumb forgot to say anything about Speck when I made my remarks. Later on in the program, however, it dawned upon me that I had forgotten to convey Speck's appreciation, so I jumped up like a jack-in-the box and asked the master of ceremonies if I could say a few more words.

I got up and my mind went blank. I stammered around and finally said:

"Speck Towns was the greatest champion and competitor I ever knew . . . I would like to hereby pay him the highest accolade that can be paid in sports: I have never known an athlete WHO COULD HOLD HIS JOCKEY STRAP."

Then I reflected on that stupid statement and quickly added: "IN FACT, I HAVE NEVER KNOWN ANYBODY WHO WOULD HAVE WANTED TO HOLD IT."

Then I reflected some more and added: "Actually, Speck was so tough that he probably didn't even wear a jockey strap . . . but he must have worn one or else he would have knocked down more hurdles than he did."

———— ■ ————

A few weeks before Speck Towns died in April, 1991, he received one of the highest compliments ever paid him. A young battalion commander with the famed 82nd Airborne Division asked the publication *Static Line*, the keeper of Airborne genealogy, to get some of the old paratroopers to write articles of mirth and morale for the troops in "Desert Storm" stationed in Saudi

Arabia. And a retired paratrooper, Col. Joseph C. Watts of Alexandria, Virginia, immediately "came through" with this heretofore untold story about Speck Towns:

"A group of elite and youthful troops is difficult to control at any time. Take 200 newly qualified U.S. Army enlisted paratroopers in the replacement pipeline, full of romping, stomping, boys full of energy and pride without their formal organization, NCOs, or officers. Leave them in a replacement depot run by 'lef' (non-parachute qualified Army personnel) while they await the call from an airborne organization, and, with those ingredients, you're just looking for trouble.

"So there we were in May, 1943, at Camp Marshal Lyautey, just north of Casablanca, Morocco, awaiting assignment. The Army officers and NCOs who ran the replacement depot were a tolerant group since many were 'Purple Heart' combat veterans of the North African campaigns. But we were 'unbloodied' and anxious for battle, and we enjoyed making life difficult for this 'lef' cadre. They had us for house-cleaning, training, and discipline, so we did our share of KP, guard, and latrine duties. However, the training was limited to PT and organized athletics.

"Each morning the camp commandant did his best to assign an NCO or officer who could 'PT' us and run us to exhaustion so we would not be capable of taking 'French Leave' for an afternoon in Casablanca or Rabat. But three hours daily of PT during May in North Africa was just not enough when it was conducted by 'lef' NCOs or officers.

"As one day followed another, so too did the instructors who mounted the PT platform to lead us through the daily dozen: push-ups, grass drills, arm circles, and jogging. None could tire us. We were fit. That's what jump school had been all about (physically fit so we would bounce, not break, when we hit the ground). Why, everyone knew jogging or running was our specialty. So each day we exhausted our instructors, not they us, and afterward we escaped into town.

"Then came that fateful day when a tall, slim officer jumped onto the PT platform and introduced himself: Captain Forrest Towns. The name didn't mean anything to me, but there was a restlessness, an undercurrent running through the knowledgeable of the troops. The rest of us were blissfully ignorant.

"The captain didn't waste time. We did some stretching exercises, then, as usual, formed into four platoons of three columns. He marched us through the camp gate and up the dusty road toward Rabat — nothing new so far. At the command, 'Double time, march,' we engaged our legs; and the smirks of the ignorant began to fade. Immediately the pace and stride were different. They were exaggerated, faster, stretched out, not the heel-toe of the paratroopers' shuffle we were accustomed to. No sir, not at all! An hour or so later our usually tight ranks had come apart. Those of us still running did so on pride alone.

"Our smugness had been left behind in the dust of the road up near Port Lyautey. It took nearly 30 minutes for our column to close on the PT area when we returned to camp. This officer beat us where we thought we were strongest (our running), and for it he gained our respect.

"During our few remaining days at Lyautey, this 'lef' (and this captain was all legs) was our leader with a capital 'L.' You guessed it: Captain Forrest Towns had run before. He had won a gold medal in the 1936 Olympics when he did the 100-meter hurdles in world record time, and he had run us like we were taking hurdles. Certainly we were better for the exercise; but most of all, we were better for the lesson in humility. The 82nd Airborne's Camp Lyautey replacements will never forget Captain Forrest Towns, wherever he is."

It was my pleasure to get in touch with Col. Watts and let him know about Coach Towns' distinguished coaching career after he had returned to Athens after his World War II service. And it was especially fun to show Speck Col. Watts' article, which he enjoyed. "Those boys needed some 'comeuppance,' " Speck recalled.

THE LEGENDARY LUMPKIN

One of the first legends I ever saw was a high school three-sport phenomenon by the name of James Quinton Lumpkin, Jr., of Lanier High in Macon, an all-state performer in football (center and fullback), basketball (guard) and track (sprints, discus and shot put).

My memory of seeing him for the first time is as vivid today as it was that spring afternoon of 1934 in the G.I.A.A. (Georgia Interscholastic Athletic Association) track meet on Georgia's old track where now is located the Tate Student Center. I was sitting in the grandstand behind Georgia's track coach and famous athletic director, Herman Stegeman, eavesdropping on his sage comments. The 220-yard dash was about to be run and Coach

Quinton Lumpkin

Stegeman was saying, "There is a big boy from Macon in this race who might be the best young athlete in the country." About that time the starter's pistol fired and they were "off." As the runners turned the curve and headed down the stretch, we watched a powerfully-built jet-black haired boy take the lead and then break the tape. It was Quinton Lumpkin.

The middle-Georgia city of Macon has turned out two athletes perhaps better known to the public—the immortal uncrowned light-heavyweight champion Young Stribling and the amazing All-America end, Vernon (Catfish) Smith. But those familiar with the record of Lumpkin would rate it more fabulous than the achievements of Strib and Catfish, who were Lump's boyhood idols.

Stories on his deeds would fill a book. During his junior year at Lanier High when the carnival came to Macon, its professional wrestler challenged anyone in the audience to a match. Lumpkin accepted and pinned the pro with the greatest of ease. The next night the carnival played nearby Gordon, Georgia, and when the wrestler made his customary challenge, who should respond but Lumpkin. Lump again scored a quick pin, following which the pro's manager called Lump aside and pleaded, "Here's 10 bucks [a lot of money then]. For Pete's sake, quit following us."

Lumpkin entered the University of Georgia in March 1935 and immediately became undisputed "King of the Campus" by winning a celebrated showdown with the heavyweight champion of the school. The "champ" had a hobby of pouring a pitcher of water from his dormitory window onto the heads of unsuspecting students walking below, then defiantly laughing in their faces. Only one person ever called the "champ's" hand. That time came when the "champ" tried his trick on Lumpkin, who immediately bounded up the stairs into the "champ's" room and demanded to know who had thrown the water. The "champ" said he didn't know and thus "lost face" and yielded his lofty position to the freshman from Macon.

But for the fact that he played at Georgia during some of the Bulldogs' darkest days in football, Lumpkin would have made All-America center. He was captain in 1938 and made the All-SEC first team. He also captained the track team, setting the school 16-pound shot put record, and was a member of Georgia's only SEC championship track team in 1937. His happiest memories of college days came from the recollection that he never lost to arch rival Georgia Tech in either football or track in freshman and varsity competition over a four-year period.

Professional football thought a great deal of Lumpkin's ability. He was the first lineman chosen in the pro draft after the 1938 season, but he refused a chance to play with the Washington Redskins. He preferred to coach at his alma mater, joining Wallace Butts' first staff as assistant freshman coach to Howell Hollis in 1939.

No man ever loved his alma mater more nor served her more loyally than Quinton Lumpkin. For a quarter of a century in Athens he distinguished himself first as a player, then as assistant freshman coach, head freshman coach, assistant varsity line coach and head varsity line coach. When his great chieftain, Wallace Butts, retired after the 1960 season, "Lump" decided it was time for him to retire, too.

Although he was a great player and an extremely valuable assistant coach to Wallace Butts, "Lump" probably will be remembered and loved the most by the football players (more than a thousand) he "looked after" in his capacity as head monitor of the Bulldogs' athletic dormitory in his day, Payne Hall. Lump and his wife, Mary, and their two sons, Jack and Jimmy, lived in Payne Hall. (Both Jack and Jimmy starred in football at old Athens High, and Jack captained Georgia's 1957 SEC championship golf team. He is now head pro at St. Simons Island, Georgia.)

"Lump" was a strict disciplinarian, but he also had a heart of gold. There is hardly a Georgia football player he didn't befriend many times, and many of them consider him the finest man they ever knew.

James Quinton Lumpkin was one in a million. Truly, he was Georgia's "Rock of Gibraltar."

"SMILEY" JOHNSON, BULLDOG AND WAR HERO

On Independence Day I never fail to remember a poor orphan boy from Clarksville, Tennessee, who won a football scholarship to Georgia in the late 1930s and made an indelible impact on

"Smiley" Johnson

everyone he ever met, especially his fellow United States Marines during World War II.

His name was Howard (Smiley) Johnson, a 160-pound freshman fullback at Georgia in 1936 who later starred as a guard under three different Bulldog coaches: Harry Mehre, 1937; Joel Hunt, 1938; and Wallace Butts, 1939, for whom he served as alternate captain.

He was nicknamed Smiley because of his unfailingly pleasant manner, and he was sent to Athens by Georgia alumnus Harold Hirsch, Jr., who owned the Coca-Cola company in Clarksville and whose father was the renowned chief legal counsel for all of Coca-Cola with headquarters in Atlanta.

In the summer of 1938, just prior to entering UGA as a freshman in the fall, it was my good fortune to be Smiley's assistant caretaker of Georgia's six old red clay tennis courts in front of LeConte Hall. He became one of my boyhood idols.

Smiley never weighed over 190 pounds as a Georgia guard, but he carried about 200 pounds when he played with the Green Bay Packers in 1940 and 1941—still quite small for a pro lineman. But his great competitive spirit easily compensated for his relatively small size.

He joined the Marine Corps after his 1941 season at Green Bay and was at Pearl Harbor as an enlisted man when the Japanese struck on December 7 that year. A year later he was at the Marine Barracks, Quantico, Virginia, enrolled in the Marines' Officer Candidates' school, and that is when I was reunited with him and saw him for the last time.

Smiley was a most unusual Marine. In addition to being a teetotaler and non-smoker, he didn't cuss and he read the Bible every night. A good example of his Christian charity occurred one evening at Quantico when we went to an off-base cafe for a milk shake, and in walked an enlisted Marine whom I recognized as movie star Tyrone Power (I had read in the paper that he was coming to Quantico as an officer candidate). But Smiley did not recognize him. This cafe was the headquarters for taxis taking Marines on liberty to nearby Washington, D.C., and that's why Power was there: to reserve a cab to visit his wife, actress Annabella.

When the taxi manager informed Power that it would require a ten dollar deposit to reserve a cab, Power said he didn't have his wallet on him. Smiley overheard and said to Power, a perfect stranger, "I'll loan you ten dollars, buddy."

Power snapped to attention when he saw the freshly commissioned 2nd Lt. Johnson, saluted him and accepted the ten-dollar bill. He obtained Smiley's barracks address and promised to repay him that very night, which he did.

"I'm surprised you didn't recognized Tyrone Power," I said to

Smiley. "He looks just like he does in the movies except his hair is cut shorter." But I should have known that Smiley probably never had seen Power in a movie. Having been a poor country boy all his life, he wasn't likely to throw away his hard-earned money on a movie.

As good a Marine as Smiley was, he had a hard time getting a commission because he was not strong in classroom work. And it must have been fate when he was "saved" by no less than the Commandant of the Marine Corps himself, who had come down from Washington to observe the Marine officer candidates in the field on a machine-gun exercise. He spotted PFC Johnson doing a superb job with his platoon, and commented to the commanding officer of the Quantico base:

"That young man will make a fine Marine officer."

"I'm afraid not, sir," said PFC Johnson's commanding officer. "He is not doing well in his classroom work and is going to flunk out."

"The hell he will," declared the Commandant. "When this class graduates, I will be here to pin the bars on him." And that's exactly what happened on March 10, 1943.

Fifteen months later "Smiley" Johnson won this country's second-highest military award—the Silver Star—for bravery under fire on Saipan. His citation read:

". . . When the enemy counter-attacked the flank position held by his platoon, 1st Lt. Johnson daringly directed the defense, exposing himself to heavy fire and helping annihilate in hand-to-hand conflict the Japanese who penetrated the position. . ."

Eight months later "Smiley" was with the 4th Marine Division (under the command of his old commanding officer at Quantico, Major General Clifton B. Cates) when it landed on Iwo Jima on D-Day, February 19, 1945. Late that afternoon when his unit was preparing defenses for the night—he personally supervising the defenses of his platoon—he was killed by exploding shell fragments when he returned to his platoon command post. His last words, spoken to a Navy corpsman seeking to tend to his wounds, were, as he pointed to four other dying Marines: "Take care of my men first."

He received a Gold Star on Iwo Jima in lieu of a second Silver Star, and he was one of nearly 6,000 Marines who died in capturing that Japanese island, which the Japanese considered impregnable and which the United States deemed necessary to take to hasten the end of the war. The Japanese fighter planes on Iwo had thwarted U.S. B-29 bombers in their efforts to bomb the Japanese mainland. After the Marines took Iwo (less than 200 of the Japanese bastion of 20,000 survived the battle), U.S. Army B-29s bombed Japan to smithereens, eventually dropped the H-bomb, and the Japanese surrendered.

Admiral Chester Nimitz, commander of U.S. Naval forces in the Pacific, said all the Marines deserved the Congressional Medal of Honor on Iwo Jima, "where uncommon valor was a common virtue."

The Marines did not forget "Smiley" Johnson. There are half a dozen athletic fields at Marine bases scattered throughout the Pacific that are named for this former Georgia Bulldog.

COSTA'S LAST STAND

I have long realized that Coach Hugh Durham knows a lot about basketball, but I didn't have any idea that he was such a student of the game's history that he knew about some of old Athens High's greatest players. But he came into my office on the morning of April 5, 1979, and said to me, "I'm glad to know that you are going to be the master of ceremonies tonight (at a banquet honoring Coach Hugh Durham's first Georgia basketball team). It's always good to have an emcee who has been a great basketball player himself."

I was a bit startled because, although I did play high school basketball at old Athens High, I really didn't make any all-star teams. By now, though, it had dawned upon me that he was pulling my leg, and the more I thought about it the more I became convinced that I should tell Coach Durham about my greatest game at old Athens High. It was back in January, 1938, up at Lavonia, Georgia. We played on the stage of the high school auditorium, and I was especially "up" for the game because my aunt and first cousins, who were natives of Lavonia, had come out to watch the contest. I later learned that they had bet their entire family fortune on Lavonia to win when they learned I was in the Athens starting lineup.

Nevertheless, I got off to a fast start—quite accidentally. I was guarding my man in the corner and all of a sudden the ball hit me in the back of the head and knocked me down and almost out. What happened was that Lavonia had a pet play of bouncing the ball off the side of the wall, which was the boundary on one side of the court (the other boundary was the orchestra pit), and I was guarding my man so closely that the ball ricocheted off the wall smack onto the back of my head. I never saw it. I went down and saw stars. I stayed down until I thought I heard the count of nine, then got up and immediately clinched the first person I saw (I had done some YMCA boxing and knew well what to do after being knocked down).

Anyway, to make a long story longer, I played out of my head the rest of the game and ended up with nine points—a lot of points in those days, the equivalent of about 50 points in today's high scoring—and we won the game, 17-16.

But, in all modesty, I must admit that game is famous not because of my performance but because of one of my teammate's never-to-be forgotten performances.

Our coach, Harrison Anderson, who had been Georgia's basketball captain the previous year, did not believe in substituting. He believed in starting five boys and letting them play the whole game. But this night one of our players, Pope Holliday (now a distinguished pediatrician in Chattanooga) pooped out; he had had pneumonia a few days before. When Pope collapsed on the floor, Coach Anderson yelled for Leo Costa to take Pope's place. Leo had not expected to play and he was not properly attired. He had on his warmup suit, but he had neglected to put on his pants because, he later told me, they were too tight and he had no idea he'd get in the game. Well, when Coach Anderson yelled, "Costa, get in the game," it frightened Leo. He instinctively pulled off his sweat jacket, then his sweat pants, and he ran to the scorer's desk clad only in his uniform jersey. Needless to say, the crowd went wild. Bob Hope nor Jack Benny ever got as many laughs as Leo did. Finally, Leo realized what they were laughing at, and he just ran off the stage all the way back to the dressing room, never to return.

Leo Costa

As would be expected, the experience had a psychological effect on Leo. He became terribly depressed and told me that he could never show his face again on the Athens high campus. I tried to console him by saying that it wasn't his face he should be ashamed of, but that seemed to do more harm than good.

Well, Leo ended up leaving town. He transferred to Baylor School in Chattanooga where he played center on the football team.

Even when he came back for the summer, he would seldom leave his home on Milledge Circle. He stayed home and practiced kicking a football in his backyard—morning and afternoon. He seemed to get relief in kicking something. Maybe he fantasized that he was kicking himself.

But there was a happy ending to this story. Leo became the greatest football placekicker in college football. He scored in every game Georgia played for four years and even scored in the Rose Bowl as Georgia beat UCLA New Year's Day, 1943.

However, he will be best remembered for his performance at Lavonia, Georgia, in January, 1938. It will always be known as "Costa's Last Stand."

Chapter Two

ATHLETES FROM MID-CENTURY

1941 - 1959

THE GREAT FRANKIE SINKWICH

The hopes of Georgia football loyalists were "sky high" when the 1941 football season began. They were counting heavily on their most ballyhooed ball-carrier since their first and only All-America halfback, the immortal Bob McWhorter in 1913. This new "wonder boy" had finished his sophomore season in impressive form, finally living up to the promise he had displayed as a freshman.

His name was Francis Frank Sinkwich, a powerfully stocky Croatian, the son of a Youngstown, Ohio, bartender who had come to the U.S. from Yugoslavia. And the preseason football magazines had hailed him as the best triple-threat halfback in the land, very likely to lead Georgia to its first Southeastern Conference football championship. But in the second game of the season against South Carolina (one of the first night games in Sanford Stadium history), Sinkwich suffered a broken jaw, which was followed by the most publicity ever given an injury in the history of American football up to that time.

The stage had been set for a pivotal battle in the Bulldogs' bid for national recognition. The Gamecocks, coached by former Georgia backfield coach Rex Enright, had upset powerful North Carolina the previous week. But Sinkwich and Company were in fine fettle and were leading comfortably, 27-6, late in the game when Sinkwich broke loose for a long gain—the play on which he received his famous and "infamous" injury.

I was a classmate and good friend of Frankie and have many times written an account of what happened. Here is the "straight dope" in Frankie's own words:

"Although the last play forced me to leave the game, I had received a hard lick to my jaw—in the same place—in the first

Frank Sinkwich

quarter on the handoff to our fullback. I carried out a fake, and the South Carolina end, Nowak, gave me a forearm to the jaw.

"On my last play of the game, though, I faked a pass and ran a good way, almost scoring. Cramps hit my legs, and I buckled. I was run out of bounds, and someone piled on, hitting my jaw again with a knee. I think it was the same Nowak. South Carolina was penalized to the one-yard line for unnecessary roughness, and we scored immediately.

"When I returned to the sidelines, Coach Butts asked me what ailed me, and I replied that I had a loose tooth. He commented: 'Oh. That's nothing!'

"It turned out to be a broken jaw. I remember spending the night at the Athens General Hospital, and the next day Speck Towns (assistant football coach and head track coach) drove me to Atlanta to see our team's orthopedic surgeon, Dr. Joe Boland (captain of the 1929 Georgia team that beat Yale in the Sanford Stadium dedicatory game). Dr. Boland sent me back to Athens to see our dentist, Dr. Jimmy Allen (whose younger brother Heyward was captain and Sinkwich's fellow tailback on the 1941 Georgia team). Dr. Allen actually had seen me right after the South Carolina game and had told me then that I had a broken jaw. Anyway, this time Dr. Allen wired my teeth together laterally.

"Now the big question was whether I could play the next week against Ole Miss (one of the best teams in the country, led by a great pair of halfbacks, Hapes and Hovious, and coached by former Georgia coach Herry Mehre. Ole Miss had beaten Georgia, 28-14, the previous year).

"Coach Butts wanted Tennessee's famous trainer, Mickey O'Brien, to examine me and recommend a protective helmet for me. So early the week of the Ole Miss game, a well-known Athens pilot, Ben Gunn, flew me to Knoxville. Mr. O'Brien telephoned his opinions to Coach Butts. I don't know what he said.

"When I returned to Athens, our trainer Fitz Lutz and Dr. Allen designed a protective helmet. However, it would not be ready until the following week when we were to play Columbia in New York City. So against Ole Miss my only protection was a chin strap of thin metal made at Basham's Machine Shop in Athens.

"With my teeth wired together, I couldn't eat solid foods. When the fans realized that I was living off soup, I received gallons and gallons of homemade soup from dozens of fans. It was mostly chicken soup. It was much more than I could eat, and the whole team drank a lot of soup at our dining room in Payne Hall that week. I also drank a lot of milk shakes—all kinds—and didn't lose any weight the whole time. I had one missing tooth, in the back, and I sucked soup and milk shakes through a straw."

Much fuss was raised over Sinkwich's injury. Charges of dirty football were leveled at South Carolina. Sinkwich, however, always refuted these charges. "I don't think it was dirty football," he said. "It simply was football, which is rough most of the time. A few days after the game I received a beautiful letter from Coach Enright apologizing for his players tackling me out of bounds after the whistle had blown."

Nevertheless, the Georgia-South Carolina series was discontinued and not renewed until 17 years later in 1958.

Sinkwich didn't have any more trouble with the jaw except during practice a day or so before the Ole Miss game. "I was running signals without the protective helmet," he recalled, "and our center, Steve Hughes, snapped the ball high and hard, and it slipped through my fingers, hitting me smack on the broken jaw. It really hurt. Coach Butts told Steve to be more careful."

Sinkwich played a whale of a game against Ole Miss despite the handicap. He said, "The worst thing was trying to breathe through wired teeth. I recall our trainer coming on the field with pliers to tighten up the wires which would get loose. There was no free substitution then, and I had to remain in the game if I wanted to continue playing."

Ole Miss took a 14-0 lead, but Georgia rallied to get a 14-14 tie. Lamar (Race Horse) Davis scored Georgia's first TD on a 45-yard reverse. Sinkwich passed to end George Poschner who lateralled to end Van Davis for the TD that enabled Leo Costa to kick the tying PAT.

The following week, the day before the Columbia game, Sinkwich finally had something to eat besides soup and milk shakes. His teeth were unwired so he could have some poached eggs.

Sinkwich went on to lead Georgia to a 9-1-1 record (losing only to Alabama in Birmingham) and the school's first bowl game. He set the NCAA rushing record of 1,103 yards and paced

Georgia to a 40-26 victory over T.C.U. in the Orange Bowl, setting a bowl record of 383 yards for total offense (9 of 13 passes for 243 yards and three TDs, plus 139 yards rushing, including a 43-yard TD jaunt).

The next year Sinkwich set the NCAA total offense record of 2,187 yards and captured the coveted Heisman trophy, which he donated to his alma mater; it now resides in the Butts-Mehre Building's Heritage Hall.

———— ■ ————

In 1943, during World War II, Frank Sinkwich and almost all his Rose Bowl teammates went into the armed services of the United States. Sinkwich joined the U.S. Marine Corps, but his physical exam at Parris Island showed him to have a heart murmur, high blood pressure, and flat feet, any of which should have disqualified him for the Marines.

"About my third day at Parris Island, while we were in the field during our boot training, I recall an ambulance arriving on the scene and I was astonished when told that it was for me. I was taken to the base hospital where I spent several days; then I was sent back to my platoon. I finished boot camp, but was then told that I was to get a physical discharge."

Sinkwich, however, continued his football career, having two fine seasons (1943 and 1944) with the Detroit Lions. He made all-pro as a rookie in 1943 and was voted the NFL's most valuable player in 1944.

"After the 1943 season," he recalls, "I took another physical exam for the service and again failed it. After the 1944 season, however, I took still another exam and passed this time."

Sinkwich then joined the Army Air Force and was put on the Second Air Force football team at Colorado Springs. While playing against the El Toro Marines, he suffered a bad knee injury that eventually ended his playing career. He was on defense preparing to tackle Elroy (Crazy) Hirsch (later a star with the Los Angeles Rams) when Bob Dove (All-America end at Notre Dame) blocked him on the knee. Ironically, Dove and Sinkwich had played on rival high school teams in Youngstown, Ohio.

Sinkwich had two knee operations, but they were not successful.

He tried to play with the old New York Yankees in 1946 and again in 1947. Then former Georgia Trainer Fitz Lutz, who had moved to the Baltimore Colts, talked him into trying out with the Colts.

"Fitz told me they would try me at T-QB" Sinkwich laughed in relating this story, "and I would not have as much strain on the knee as a running back. But they played me at fullback and mostly at defensive halfback. And the knee wouldn't hold up."

So Frankie returned to Athens for a couple of years, beginning his career as a beer distributor. But football called him back as head coach at Tampa University, where he had a successful tenure for several years. Ultimately though, his love for Georgia brought him back "home" to Athens.

Frank Sinkwich was an easy choice for the College Hall of Fame, and he no doubt would have made the Pro Hall of Fame were it not for the knee injury. He was a genuine *super* player, and throughout his business career in Athens he was a *super* supporter of anything involving his alma mater. He and Bill Hartman were the co-chairmen of the fund drive for the Butts-Mehre Building, the Taj Mahal of college athletic offices.

When Sinkwich died October 22, 1990, following a long bout with cancer, President Charles Knapp ordered the University's flag on Herty Drive lowered to half-mast—a rare tribute to an alumnus.

GEORGIA'S ITALIAN STALLION

Charley Trippi, the original Italian Stallion, was the best all-around football player I ever saw, counting offense and defense—60 minutes every big game. He made many spectacular plays. His greatest, I say, was against Alabama in Sanford Stadium late in the season of 1946. Both teams were undefeated and it was a titanic struggle. Trippi went back to punt on third down, as was the custom in those days when deep in your own territory. Alabama blocked the kick and three Alabama boys beat Trippi to the free ball and fell on it. But Trippi dove into the pile and guess who came up with the ball? It was Trippi. On the next play, now fourth down, Trippi punted out of danger and he went on to lead Georgia to a great 14-0 victory and an undefeated season, capped by a win over Charley (Choo Choo) Justice and North Carolina in the Sugar Bowl.

In that same Alabama game, on Trippi's 40-yard touchdown run that clinched matters, I was holding the chain (the 10-yard marker) on the sidelines along with the Alabama chain-holder, a distinguished lawyer from Birmingham, who had been captain

Charley Trippi

Dan Magill working the chains

of one of Alabama's first teams in the 1890s. He was a little fellow well into his 70s. I got so excited that I ran down the sidelines with Trippi, dragging the distinguished Alabama chainholder, who was cussing me from here to Kingdom come. That episode caused the rules to be changed the next year so that only a bona fide official—in striped uniform—could handle the chains.

A special place in Bulldog history is reserved for those players who never lost to "The Enemy," starting with Bob McWhorter, Georgia's first All-American, who led Georgia over Georgia Tech four straight years in 1910-11-12-13. He ended a seven-game winning streak by Tech and he also was mainly responsible for Georgia being the only team ever to beat Tech's famous coach John Heisman four straight years.

Heisman Trophy Winner Frank Sinkwich led Georgia to three straight wins over Tech in 1940-41-42. Francis Tarkenton did it in 1958-59-60. Andy Johnson likewise in 1971-2-3.

There were numerous Bulldogs on Coach Dooley's first five teams at Georgia (1964 through 1968) who never lost to Tech, and also on his teams from 1978 through 1983 (six years in a row), notably QB Buck Belue (four times) and Herschel Walker (three times) who scored nine touchdowns against Tech.

But perhaps the greatest star ever in this ancient series was the scintillating Sicilian, Charley Trippi.

Charley was a sophomore in 1942 in his first varsity game against Tech in Athens. He had begun the season as backup for All-America tailback Frankie Sinkwich. But at the season's end Coach Butts wanted both Trippi and Sinkwich in the same backfield. So he moved Sinkwich to fullback and elevated Trippi to the No. 1 triple-threat position of tailback.

The 1942 game was the biggest in the history of Southern football. Tech was undefeated and Georgia was 9-1, having been upset by Auburn the previous week and knocked out of its No. 1 national ranking. Nevertheless, the Rose Bowl committee said the winner of this game would receive the bid to visit Pasadena New Year's Day.

Georgia won easily, 34-0, thanks to two touchdown passes by Trippi plus an 87-yard touchdown run after a fake pass. A few weeks later Trippi was voted the outstanding player as Georgia beat UCLA in the Rose Bowl, 9-0.

Trippi went into the Air Force after the Rose Bowl game and returned to Georgia after World War II, late in the season of 1945. He immediately resumed his Tech-beating act with an incredible performance on Grant Field. He handled the ball 42 times and gained 517 yards and also punted twice—first to the Tech 10 and then to the nine. He rushed 12 times for 62 yards, completed 12 of 23 passes for 321 yards, returned six punts for 114 yards, one interception for 21 yards.

He closed out his career against Tech in 1946 in Athens with three TDs running and one passing.

Overall against Tech Trippi ran for 5 TDs and passed for six —11 touchdowns in three games.

No wonder Tech's legendary coach Bobby Dodd called Charley Trippi the greatest player he had ever seen.

REID PATTERSON GETS MAD

The University of Georgia's only Olympic swimmer and NCAA champion was a six-foot-four, raw-boned, blond Kentuckian by the name of Logan Reid Patterson, who learned to swim in a river at the age of six but never saw a swimming race until he entered Georgia's forestry school as a freshman in September, 1950.

A direct descendent of Benjamin Logan, who came in with Daniel Boone to settle southeastern Kentucky, Patterson did not take part in any athletics at Pineville, Kentucky, high school. His only competitive endeavors in those days were in outdoor contests involving Boy Scouts, in which he attained Eagle rank, and the district high school music contest in which he earned excellent rating in piano.

It must have been fate when this tall mountaineer caught the attention of Georgia swimming coach B. W. (Bump) Gabrielsen while "cooling off" in Stegeman pool on the Georgia campus one hot September day in 1950. The shrewd Minnesota Norwegian, who developed the New York lassie Gloria Callen to a world's record in the backstroke, detected tremendous potential in the long, sweeping strokes of Patterson as he swam around that day.

Gabrielsen first trained Patterson in the backstroke because he needed a backstroker, already having the best freestyle sprinter in the SEC in Charley Cooper of Augusta and the best breaststroker in Charley Guyer of Savannah. And, even though

Patterson placed fifth in both the NCAA 100- and 200-yard back-stroke events at Princeton in 1952, Gabrielsen decided in the summer of 1952 that Patterson's best event would be the freestyle sprints. That winter at Fort Lauderdale Patterson won the 50-meter freestyle in the East-West meet, upsetting the favorite, Michigan's big Don Hill, holder of the national collegiate 50-yard long course record.

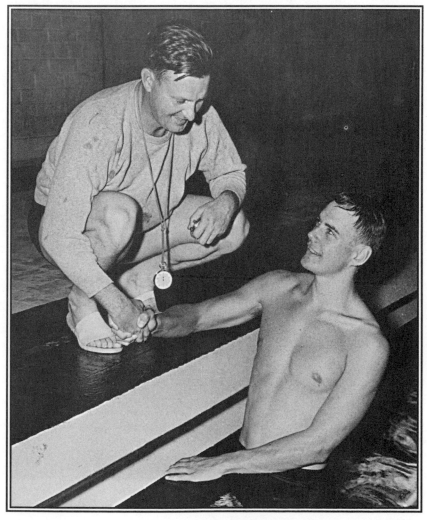

Coach "Bump" Gabrielsen with star swimmer Reid Patterson

The last of March found Patterson at the 1953 NCAAs at the Ohio State natatorium in Columbus. "Bump" thought his boy would win both the 50 and 100 (he had secretly broken the American records in both events in practice, but he was still relatively inexperienced). He "goosed" the turn on the 50 and failed to qualify for the finals. Patterson was so depressed that "Bump" knew he had to do something drastic to get him up for the 100 the next day.

"What I am about to do will hurt me more than it will Patterson," he told me (I had accompanied them to Columbus). "But I had rather have him mad at me and the world than have him feeling sorry for himself. He can win that 100 if he can regain his spirit."

Whereupon Gabrielsen looked up Patterson and bawled him out: "Still a rookie! Fastest sprinter in the country and you'll be sitting in the stands tonight. Get back in that pool and count every piece of tile in your lane. You are going to get acquainted with the end of the pool. I don't want you to be startled when you reach it tomorrow. It won't bite you."

The hot-tempered Patterson became so angry he didn't speak another word until a few minutes before the trials of the 100 the next afternoon. He won his heat in 50.8 seconds, and he won the finals in 50.5 seconds in a sensational race, all six men hitting the finish of the first, second and third laps simultaneously with the capacity crowd of 1,800 on its feet screaming. Patterson took the lead going home and was increasing it at the finish.

Pupil and coach happily embraced seconds later. All was well again, and it was a jubilant ride back to Athens.

BIG JIM WHATLEY

Bobby Walden, the Big Toe of Cairo, was a great kicker of footballs. But he was not Georgia's greatest kicker. That honor belongs to Big Jim Whatley, perhaps the University of Alabama's finest all-around athlete, who spent nearly three decades coaching baseball, football and basketball at Georgia.

Big Jim could perform many unusual feats of athletic prowess.

One of his best tricks was to touch the molding at the top of a door's entrance with his foot. He also could kick out light bulbs in the ceiling of a room. That was one of his most spectacular tricks and it scared the daylights out of many an unsuspecting person.

In the 1950s, whenever Georgia had an outstanding football prospect in town, I would try to impress him with the wonders on the campus. And inevitably the prospect would wind up at

Jim Whatley

Stegeman Hall (home of the athletic department then) to see Big Jim kick the top of the door. You'd be surprised at the number of recruits we got in this manner.

Big Jim really is a modest fellow when it comes to his own accomplishments, but he used to be downright conceited when it came to bragging about his old bird dog, Ned. All of us at the athletic department had heard so much about the wonders of Ned that we were fed up. One day I challenged Jim. I told him that when I worked on the *Atlanta Journal*, I had covered the National Field Trials at Waynesboro and that I would like to see how Ned compared to those real champions. Undaunted, Big Jim said that even though Ned had never participated in field trials, he was far better than any of those "show dogs" and he would be glad to prove it even though Ned was old and past his prime.

Not long after that, Jim invited me to go hunting with him and Ned. I must admit that I was disappointed when I first saw Ned, who not only was past his prime but had at least one paw in the grave. However, like a mother with her child, Jim seemed unaware of any of the dog's imperfections. We spent a long afternoon walking through field after field, but making very slow progress since Ned had to sit down and rest every 10 yards. We walked for hours without Ned ever pointing a single bird. The crowning blow came late in the afternoon when finally Coach Whatley himself flushed a covey that flew across a creek. Giving the credit to Ned, who had done absolutely nothing, Jim encouraged Ned to "do his thing." Eagerly Jim and I approached the creek ready to cross—but not Ned. As long as I live, I shall never forget Big Jim imploring Ned to cross the creek—all in vain. Finally, Big Jim had to stoop down, pick up champion Ned and carry him across the creek in his arms. But the next morning, Jim simply explained it by saying, "Ned had an off day just like any champion occasionally does."

———— ■ ————

On legendary Adolph Rupp's last appearance in old Woodruff Hall, Georgia scored a sensational upset, 71-60, on January 17, 1950. Adolph had a good team, too, led by native Georgian Big Bill Spivey at center, and they won the conference tournament at the end of the season.

Anyway, the Georgia team that whipped Kentucky in Woodruff Hall in 1950 was coached by Big Jim, before he settled in as coach of the Bulldog baseball team. And Coach Whatley loved to tell about a five-dollar bet he won from Coach Rupp.

The story begins back in 1947 in Jasper, Indiana, when Whatley entertained Coach Rupp for three hours by just *listening* to Rupp talk. In the course of the conversation Coach Rupp stated that he would resign from coaching basketball within five years, or by 1952. Well, when Rupp made that statement, Whatley immediately bet him five dollars that he'd still be coaching in five years. Rupp accepted the wager.

Whatley had to wait patiently 14 years for an opportunity to collect his five dollars. It happened in June 1961, while he was sitting in the Kansas City airport. He saw Rupp walk by and stop at a desk to purchase some additional insurance. When the insurance attendant placed a five-dollar bill in change in front of Rupp on the counter, Whatley reached around and covered the bill with his big hand and said:

"Coach Rupp, this is payment for the bet we made in 1947. Will you please autograph it for me?"

The amazed Rupp replied, "Why, sure Jim, you damned bounty hunter, it looks like I'll be coaching forever."

Coach Whatley now has that five-dollar bill framed and hanging in his office.

———— ◼ ————

Big Jim loves to go fishing, and he especially loves to tell fishing stories. One of his favorites is about the time he went fishing on Owl Creek in Florida with his longtime friend and Georgia alumnus John Turner McAllister of Dothan, Alabama, and fellow Georgia coaches Perron Shoemaker and Forrest (Speck) Towns.

Big Jim, incidentally, was called Big Jim from the day he was born in Tuscaloosa, Alabama. He was an 11 1/2-pounder at birth (weighed on fish scales no doubt), and he was six feet tall by the time he was 14. Rising to 6-6 in height during his college days as an all-star tackle on a Rose Bowl championship team at

Alabama (Bear Bryant played end next to him), he was truly a giant of a man.

Well, on this particular fishing trip on Owl Creek, Whatley and his party started out with a minimum of gas in their boat, but they decided to risk it, nevertheless (although Whatley still claims he warned Shoemaker that they would run out of gas). Finally, when the motor sputtered into silence, they spotted a pick-up truck over on the bank and proceeded to "borrow it" without the absent owner's permission. After all, the owner had been kind enough to leave the keys in the truck.

Shoemaker and Towns hopped in the truck and left Whatley at the scene to explain things to the truck owner should he return before they did. As luck would have it, the owner did return shortly thereafter. He looked for his missing truck, then he looked up the hill overlooking the creek, and there was Big Jim hovering above him. As their eyes met, Big Jim hollered down to the stranger, "We borrowed your truck to get some gas. We didn't think you'd mind."

The stranger didn't say anything. He just went about unloading his boat. Finally, Shoemaker and Towns returned with his truck, and Shoemaker went up to the stranger and again explained, "We borrowed your truck. Hope you didn't mind."

Up to that point the stranger had not said a word, but now he shot back at Shoemaker:

"I can plainly see that you 'borrowed' my truck, and I don't mind that so much; but what I do mind is that you left the biggest S.O.B. I've ever seen to tell me about it."

——— ■ ———

Coach Whatley once had a player who probably had never been to Sunday school in his life, much less read the bible. He happened to be the star hitter on the team that season and, during an interview with a sportswriter, he told the gullible reporter that his hitting success was due to his being highly religious.

"I give all the credit to the Lord," the star player said. Well, when this story came out in the paper, Coach Whatley was infuriated. He went up to the player the next day at practice in front of the whole team and said: "————, this story is an outrage.

You are not a religious man—far from it. In fact, I bet you have never been in church. I'll put up $20.00 right now that you can't recite the Lord's Prayer."

The boy immediately pulled out his wallet—he was scared to leave it in the locker room—and he covered Coach Whatley's $20.00 bill.

Whereupon Coach Whatley demanded, "All right. Let's hear you recite the Lord's Prayer."

The boy did not hesitate. He began, "Now I lay me down to sleep, I pray the Lord my soul to keep."

The startled Whatley interrupted him, handed him the money and apologized: "I could have sworn you didn't know it."

———— ■ ————

For many summers Coach Whatley and his wife, Mae, vacationed at Sanibel Island on the Gulf Coast of Florida. While Big Jim would go fishing, usually for snook, Mrs. Whatley searched for sea shells to add to her fine collection.

One time Big Jim had a frightening encounter with a 10-foot alligator while fishing. He immediately fetched a rifle from his car, returned and pumped two shots between the gator's eyes. Thinking the gator dead, Big Jim picked up the monster and put it in the trunk of his car, then rode down the beach a few miles to find Mrs. Whatley.

When he reached Mrs. Whatley, he excitedly yelled for her to come to the car. He told her that he had discovered a gigantic and beautiful sea shell and it was in the trunk of the car. Mrs. Whatley waited eagerly for Big Jim to reveal the treasure, but just as soon as he opened the trunk the very-much-alive alligator opened its jaws wide and snapped viciously at his tormentor. Big Jim responded with one of his greatest athletic maneuvers; he slammed down the trunk and did a handstand on top of it to keep it down.

Big Jim later learned that shooting an alligator between the eyes does not kill it, merely stuns it, and that it is necessary to shoot it several inches back of its head, where its brain is located, to kill it.

Anyway, before Coach Whatley could get an expert to kill the gator, it completely destroyed the trunk of his car by whipping the stuffings out of it with its tail.

Conrad Manisera and the Double Exchange

The Southeastern Conference punt return record of 100 yards was set on Vanderbilt's Dudley Field Saturday afternoon, September 20, 1952, in a season opener that Georgia won, 19-7.

This team was one of Wallace Butts' finest offensive machines, averaging 170.7 yards per game passing. It lacked the line material to develop a strong running game and a good defense, but it really had the passing talent, what with Zeke Bratkowski pitching to All-America ends Harry Babcock and John Carson. All three later played in the NFL.

But there were two other players on that team who were equally brilliant in their specialty: the always-thrilling punt return. In those days it was the fashion on punt returns to employ two safety men in a double exchange. The player receiving the punt could fake the ball on the exchange or he could keep it. Georgia's backfield coach, Sterling DuPree (the fastest football player in the South at Auburn in the early 1930s), was one of the best coaches in the business in teaching the double-safety return, and he had two genuine speed merchants to coach: Conrad Manisera, the Jersey Jet who had taken part in the 1948 U.S. Olympic 400-meter tryouts, and Jimmy Campagna, the Rochester Rocket.

Manisera actually was the more dangerous runner of the two (on a double exchange with Zippy Morocco against Alabama in 1951 he had gone 72 yards).

Let Coach DuPree recall this record-setting 100-yard return vs. Vanderbilt:

"The play had been set up by Manisera's two fine returns of 20 and 56 yards in the first quarter, and we had telephoned from our coaches' booth in the press box down to Coach Bill Hartman on the sidelines to have Manisera fake the next punt return and give to Campagna. Midway the second quarter the Vandy kicker got off a long punt that Manisera fielded in the end zone. Of course, no punt should be fielded in the end zone. The rule usually is not to

Conrad Manisera

field any kick inside the 10 yard line. But Conrad caught it in the left corner of the end zone and he and Campagna made a perfect exchange. Manisera did a beautiful fake, running to his right and drawing most of the Vandy players to him. Campagna simply ran straight up the left sidelines 100 yards. He had a block or two, but he really didn't need much help."

A few weeks later Campagna and Manisera pulled their act

again vs. Pennsylvania in Philadelphia, Campagna going 67 yards "all the way." But there was a sad ending to that story. Many of Manisera's kinfolks had come over from New Jersey to see Connie perform, and Campagna was supposed to let Manisera have the ball on this particular exchange. After the game, one of Manisera's kinfolks teased Conrad, saying:

"We thought you were the beega star. But you never getta the ball. You not the star. You the dummy."

It so infuriated the already chagrined Manisera that he quit the team and went into the Army for four years. But he did return to Georgia in 1955, and although a bit overweight, he was good enough to start at left halfback and he scored an early touchdown against Ole Miss in the opener, showing his old-time speed on a right end sweep.

But Coach Butts never again used him in the double-safety punt return.

LONG JOHN CARSON

Another of the Georgia Bulldogs' incredibly versatile athletes was Long John Carson, the namesake and grandson of the nation's first famous "country music" star, Fiddlin' John Carson. But when Fiddlin' John was in his prime back in the 1920s and 1930s, his music was known as "mountain music" or "hillbilly music."

"I well remember my granddad," Long John told me on one of our numerous interviews when he was starring for Georgia in four sports in the early 1950s. "I've seen him play his old fiddle many a time. His great-grandfather, Allan Carson, brought it over from Ireland back in the 1700s, and it was said to have been made by the son of the late Italian violin maker, Antonio Stradivari.

"I also used to enjoy listening to his daughter, Rosa Lee, sing hillbilly songs." She was the Loretta Lynn of her day, frequently accompanying Fiddlin' John on his performances throughout the country.

Fiddlin' John is perhaps best remembered by Georgians for the prominent part he played in the political campaigns of Eugene Talmadge, famous father of Senator Herman Talmadge in the 1930s and 1940s.

Recalls Long John: "He'd go from town to town with Gene, and he would get up on top of a flat-bottom truck in the courthouse square and play his fiddle for the country folk an hour or so to get them primed for Gene's speeches. Aunt Rosa Lee, whose stage name was Moonshine Kate, also would sing and buck-and-wing dance. I remember one of the songs abut Gene went like this: 'I've got a Eugene dog, I've got a Eugene cat. I'm

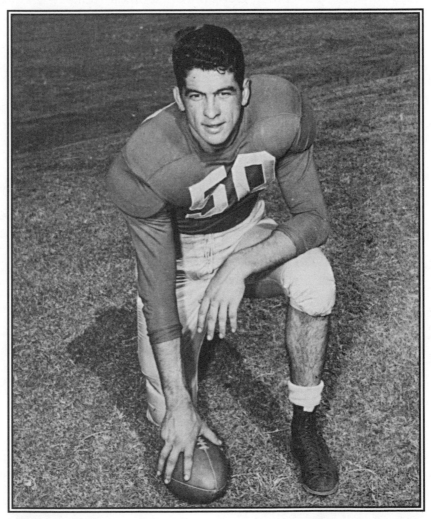

Long John Carson

a Talmadge man from my shoes to my hat.'"

My first observation of Long John Carson was in the late 1940s when he was starring in football, basketball, baseball and golf for old Roosevelt High in Atlanta. I was prep editor for the *Atlanta Journal,* and I gave him the nickname, "Long John" (apologies to Robert Louis Stevenson and his Long John Silver). I also recommended him for a scholarship to Georgia, and John entered the university as a freshman in the fall of 1949, the same year I came back home as Coach Butts' sports information director.

Long John was Georgia's last four-letter athlete, excelling in football (end), basketball (forward), baseball (first base) and golf (he reached the quarter finals of the NCAA golf tournament in the days when it was match play instead of medal play).

Carson made All-America in football his senior season (1953), setting the school record of 45 catches as the favorite target of All-America quarterback Zeke Bratkowski. This record stood 16 years until Charley Whittemore busted it with 46 catches in 1969, and Carson probably would still hold the record except for the fact he was injured on the opening kickoff in the season's final game against Georgia Tech. Coach Butts utilized Carson's ball-carrying ability by letting him return kickoffs, and on this particular play against Tech he was about to break into an open field when he pulled a muscle trying to sidestep the last Yellow Jacket defender. But he still led the SEC as a receiver for the second straight year, and in fact led the nation that year.

Long John Carson played six years for the Washington Redskins, making the pro bowl in 1958. He finished his playing career in 1960, helping Houston win the first AFL title. Then he spent a long time scouting for Philadelphia and Minnesota, frequently coming back to Sanford Stadium on scouting missions.

There's no doubt that Fiddlin' John Carson would have been mighty proud of his namesake.

THE AMAZING ZIPPY MOROCCO

Anthony (Zippy) Morocco came South from Youngstown, Ohio, on a football scholarship (and he was one of the best kick returners and pass-receivers in Bulldog history), but he was elected to the State of Georgia's Sports Hall of Fame because of his amazing basketball exploits his senior season of 1953.

Football in the fall and sometimes in January and February (spring practice) limited Zippy's basketball career at Georgia. He was able to play only one full season and he had to come back to school a fifth year to do it. But it was well worth the trouble. The little guard (only 5-10, 165-pounds) set three Southeastern Conference scoring records and was voted the league's Most Valuable Player (the only other Georgia player to receive that honor was Dominique Wilkins in 1981).

He scored 590 points in 25 games (23.6 average), breaking the old record of 540 points in 26 games by Kentucky's All-American, Cliff Hagan, in 1952. He set a record of 210 free throw points.

Zippy Morocco

There's no telling how many records he would have broken had he been able to play three full seasons for the Bulldogs (freshmen weren't eligible for the varsity in those days, so he couldn't play four seasons as they do nowadays).

His most memorable performance came on the night of February 25, 1953, at Knoxville, Tennessee, when he scored a Bulldog record 38 points to pace a sensational Georgia upset over Tennessee, 87-86.

The next morning, at my sports information office in Georgia's old athletic offices atop Memorial Hall, I received a telephone call from my counterpart at Tennessee, Gus Manning, who excitedly reported to me:

"I just want to tell you that your Zippy Morocco last night gave the greatest performance I have ever seen on a Tennessee court. It may sound crazy to you, me being a Tennessee man and calling you about a Georgia player, but after a performance like that I think credit ought to go where credit is due. I'm just telling you, I've never seen anything like it on a basketball court.

"Our coach, Emmett Lowery, says it was the greatest performance he ever saw by anybody—and Coach Lowery was an All-American at Purdue in the Big 10.

"Morocco finished with 38 points, and when he broke Cliff Hagan's all-time All-SEC scoring record late in the game, time was called and an announcement was made on our PA system, following which the Tennessee fans gave Morocco the biggest ovation I've ever heard.

"The amazing thing about Morocco was the distance of his set shots. He was hitting from out around the center line, 35 and 40 feet from the basket. Our defense was driving him out, stopping his pet shot—the drive to the basket—and he had to take his chances from almost the middle of the court.

"He put on his greatest exhibition in the last few minutes. Georgia was behind by a point, and the team started freezing the ball to kill time for a last shot. With five seconds left the ball was flipped to Morocco and he knocked the bottom out of the basket from about 40 feet out. It beat us 87-86. It was without a doubt the greatest set shot performance we ever saw at Tennessee."

Those were the days when the players made two-handed shots, not the one-handed push shots of basketball today. And, practically all of his set shots in those days would have been three-pointers today.

Also, in those days it was not against the rules to freeze the ball to protect a lead late in the game, and I did see Zippy and little Joe Jordan put on perhaps the greatest "freeze" in Georgia basketball history. It enabled Georgia to beat arch rival Georgia Tech in its own backyard in the "rubber" game of a three-game series, February 7, 1951. Little Joe (then a senior and an all-SEC ball-hawking guard) and Zippy (then a sophomore) were fantastic with their dribbling dexterity and cat-like quickness in protecting a 54-53 Georgia lead the last two minutes of the game.

In those days, if a player was fouled by the team trying to stop a "freeze," the fouled team had a choice of attempting a free throw or taking the ball out of bounds. Tech players couldn't get close enough to Zippy or Joe to foul them, but they did twice foul other Georgia players, and Georgia Coach Jim Whatley each time chose to take the ball out of bounds. He knew Zippy and Joe would continue their uncanny control of the ball, which they did in all-star style.

Zippy Morocco has remained in Athens following his graduation and has become a successful businessman and solid citizen in the community. Several years ago he took up tennis and was developing into an outstanding player, but an old football leg injury recurred and has limited his play. He is very proud of his son Chris's football record at Clemson (he quarterbacked the Tigers to the ACC crown a few years ago). Zippy also gets a big kick out of criticizing his close friend, fellow Bulldog immortal Charley Trippi, on the golf course at the Athens Country Club.

It was Trippi, the original Italian Stallion, who clinched Zippy's decision to attend Georgia instead of Ohio State. Coach Butts had Trippi, the year he led the Chicago Cardinals to the NFL title in 1947, sell Zippy on Georgia. It was impossible for a young Italian-American to turn down the USA's most famous Italian-American athlete of the day.

THUNDERING THERON SAPP

I have known many athletes who had to overcome adversity to reach their goals, but perhaps the "cake-taker" was a middle-Georgian, born in Dublin and reared in nearby Macon, by the name of Theron Coleman Sapp.

He played four years at left halfback under the legendary Selby Buck at Lanier High in Macon. He led the Poets to 11 straight victories his senior season in 1953, his team losing a 9-6 state title game to Grady High of Atlanta, coached by Erk Russell, who 10 years later began his illustrious career as Georgia's "Secretary of Defense."

Sapp was a much-sought-after prospect by all the leading football schools in the South. He signed a grant-in-aid to Georgia, but an accident in the spring of 1954 almost ended his football career. He hurt his neck diving into a swimming pool (hit the

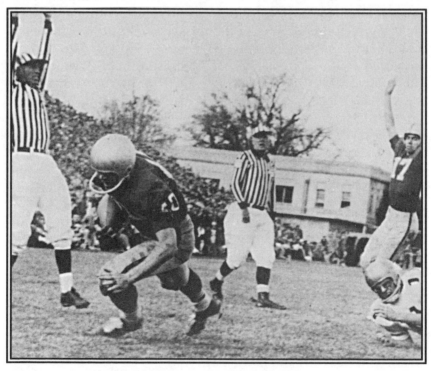

Theron Sapp breaking the drought

bottom) and reinjured it in the high school all-star practices in Atlanta in August. An examination then showed him to have fractured a vertebrae.

Georgia Coach Wallace Butts was as crestfallen as Sapp, but he told Sapp that his scholarship was still good at Georgia and that he could earn his keep as a manager.

Sapp's neck was placed in a cast during his freshman year, but he still dreamed of playing football again. He asked Coach Butts for permission to take part in spring practice 1955, and he played on the B team that fall. Then, in spring practice 1956, he let Coach Butts know that he was ready to be his No. 1 fullback. In the G-Day game he was the top rusher with 123 yards on 18 carries, but old man Tough Luck again reared his ugly head in the fall. An injury sidelined Sapp and he had to play No. 4 fullback.

But the determined Sapp won the starting job in 1957, rushing for 599 yards on 137 carries, the most yardage by a Bulldog since Billy Mixon in 1950, and he earned All-SEC honors. He repeated as All-SEC fullback in 1958.

It was in the last game of 1957 that Sapp's great play against Georgia Tech on Grant Field in Atlanta earned him Georgia Bulldog immortality. Georgia had lost eight straight games to "The Enemy" but Sapp, who backed up the line on defense, recovered a Tech fumble at midfield in the third quarter and then almost single-handedly led a 50-yard TD drive, carrying nine times (six times in succession). When he scored the game's winning TD from the one on fourth down, ending the eight-year losing streak, Georgia Bulldog Poet Laureate Harold M. Walker penned his famous poem, "The Man Who Broke the Drought."

In 1960 the Philadelphia Eagles won the world's championship of professional football, and guess who was their bread-and-butter ball-carrier? It was a big, blond boy from Macon, Georgia, who doctors had said in 1954 would never again play football.

THE MAN WHO BROKE THE DROUGHT

You can rave about your Sinkwich
And Trippi's praises sing,
While talk about the "Bowl Days"
Still makes the welkin ring.

But to all Bulldog supporters
In every precinct in the South,
I propose a hearty toast
To the man who broke the drouth!

Rise up you loyal Georgians
From Tybee Light to Rabun Gap,
Here's to the Macon Mauler,
The mighty Theron Sapp.

I have seen some lovely paintings
In galleries of art,
Gorgeous sunsets on the water
Which stirred the inner heart.

But of all the wondrous visions
Ever seen by eyes of mine,
I'll take old number forty
Crashing through that Jacket line.

And so down through the ages
Whenever Bulldogs meet,
Whether in the peaceful countryside
Or on a crowded street,

The word will still be carried
By every loyal mouth—
Let's stand and drink another toast
To the man who broke the drouth!

by Harold Walker

KING JAMES (ORR)

There have been plenty of so-called "sleepers" in sports. That is, unheralded players who came from nowhere to attain stardom status.

Perhaps the "sleepingest sleeper" in Bulldog football history was a young man who came to Georgia from Seneca, South Carolina, without a scholarship.

The son of the town doctor, he had played only one year of high school football. Basketball was his forte. He had made all-state twice in that sport.

When Georgia opened the 1955 season against Ole Miss in Atlanta, this boy was not expected to play, but injuries to the right halfback corps forced Coach Wallace Butts to put him in the line-up in the second quarter. He immediately responded by catching a 46-yard touchdown pass from quarterback Dick Young.

And he went on to lead the Southeastern Conference in receiving his very first season.

His name: James Edward Orr.

Jimmy Orr repeated as the SEC's leading receiver his senior year in 1957, and he was rookie-of-the-year at Pittsburgh in 1958. He twice made all-pro and played in two Super Bowls for Baltimore in 1968 and 1970, being a favorite receiver for the great Johnny Unitas.

Jimmy Orr made many splendid catches as a Georgia Bulldog,

Jimmy Orr (right) with Johnny Unitas

but the one I remember best and consider his most important reception was against Georgia Tech in Atlanta in the last game of 1957. Thundering Theron Sapp appropriately is remembered as the Georgia hero that day when the Bulldogs "broke the drought." But it wouldn't have happened had not Jimmy Orr made a great catch on the winning TD drive.

It was third down and 12 at the Tech 39 when Charley Britt faded back and hit Jimmy Orr on the sidelines for a 13-yard gain and a first down by inches.

Jimmy Orr was named for the great Scottish king, James the Sixth, and Jimmy Orr was the king of Bulldog receivers. In three years wearing the Red and Black, *Jimmy Orr never dropped a single pass!*

PAT DYE

He was not big for a defensive guard (only 200 pounds) but he was as fast as most of the halfbacks in his day, and he was absolutely one of the most colorful and very best defensive players who ever starred in the Southeastern Conference.

He hailed from a little country town in Richmond County, Blythe, near Augusta. His name was Patrick Fain Dye, the youngest of three brothers who were first-string linemen at Georgia. Wayne and Nat preceded him.

As a sophomore in 1958 Pat Dye made one of the most spectacular plays in Sanford Stadium history. It was against Kentucky and occurred when the Wildcats' All-SEC halfback, Calvin Bird, was running up the field with a kickoff. Dye, instead of tackling Bird, simply stripped the ball from him at the Kentucky 25 and raced into the end zone for a touchdown!

The next season (1959) in a big game against Florida in Jacksonville, Dye helped stop a deep Gator penetration by deflecting a Florida pass that Georgia safety man Charley Britt intercepted and returned 100 yards to goal.

The very next week, in one of the most famous games in Georgia annals, Dye set the stage for Francis Tarkenton's immortal TD pass that won the SEC championship. Auburn held a 13-7

Pat Dye

lead with three minutes left on the clock when Dye recovered a Bryant Harvard fumble, following which Tarkenton led a TD drive that won the game, 14-13.

Ironically, Dye later coached Auburn 12 years and piloted the Tigers to four SEC championships.

In his final game for Georgia in 1960 against Georgia Tech in Sanford Stadium, Pat Dye preserved a thrilling 7-6 Bulldog victory by blocking a Tech PAT kick by Tommy Wells. Pat lined up at defensive right end (instead of guard) on that play, and he painfully blocked the kick with his face. After the game, when a sportswriter asked him about blocking the kick with his face, Pat replied:

"It tasted mighty good."

THE PEERLESS PILOT

It was a hometown boy, Bob McWhorter of Athens, who led Georgia out of the football wilderness in 1910 (five straight losses to John Heisman-coached Georgia Tech teams); and it was another Athens boy who led the Bulldogs out of the doldrums and back to the throne room in 1959.

This boy grew up only a stone's throw from where McWhorter used to run down rabbits in his father's cotton fields.

He was a born quarterback, starting his career at the Athens YMCA, then playing four years as the starting QB at old Athens High, leading Athens to the state championship over perennial power Valdosta in the title game played in Sanford Stadium.

The next year, as a Georgia freshman, he led the Bullpups to a perfect season, running and passing the Pups to victory over a previously unbeaten Georgia Tech yearling team on Grant Field just 48 hours before Theron Sapp keyed Georgia's first victory over Tech in eight years.

And, in 1958, when he was finally able to play on the Georgia varsity, no player ever had a tougher assignment in his varsity debut, nor has any player ever responded with a more brilliant performance.

It was the opening game against the powerful Texas Longhorns in their own pasture in Austin with Georgia trailing 7-0 late in the third quarter and a Texas quick-kick having rolled dead on the Georgia 5-yard line. That's when Coach Wallace Butts first inserted Tarkenton into the lineup. Tarkenton immediately directed a 95-yard touchdown drive that required 21 plays and consumed nine minutes. This magnificent drive culminated with Tarkenton passing three yards to Jimmy Vickers for a

TD, then Tarkenton went for broke. He hit end Aaron Box for the two-point conversion and Georgia led, 8-7.

As a junior in 1959 the preacher's son (Tarkenton was named for the famous Methodist bishop, Francis Asbury) led Georgia to its first SEC title in 11 years, but he never started a single game that season! Coach Butts, imitating Coach Shug Jordan's "X and Y" two-team system used at Auburn in 1953, employed a similar

Coach Butts and Francis Tarkenton with SEC championship trophy, 1959.

two-team lineup at Georgia. Coach Butts had Charley Britt, one of his favorite players, as the returning no. 1 quarterback in 1959, and he had the brilliant junior quarterback, Francis Tarkenton, who was good enough to be a regular if any junior ever was anywhere. So, with Solomon-like wisdom, Coach Butts decided to use the two-team system, and he came up with two teams of equal strength, and the players played both offense and defense in those days. There was Britt's team and Tarkenton's team, and they played about equal time every game.

Coach Butts thought he had material good enough to make a run for the SEC title, but he had a very tough schedule, especially tough with Alabama in the opening game. Bear Bryant was in his second season back at his alma mater, and he really believed he could be national champion in 1959. And Bear would have been national champion in 1959 had he not lost the opener against Georgia; he won all his other games.

Guess who led Georgia to a sensational upset over the Bear?

It was Francis Tarkenton, who engineered both Georgia TD drives in a great 17-3 victory. He took the 'Dogs 80 yards to goal in the second quarter and 75 yards in the final period. His favorite receiver was a big, rangy end from Atlanta, Gordon Kelley, who later was a fine defensive end in the NFL. On this day Kelley caught five passes from Tarkenton, three on crucial third-down plays.

Against Alabama Tarkenton completed six of seven passes, and the one incomplete was dropped. Incidentally, Tarkenton was the most accurate passer I have ever seen. In 1959 he completed 60.8 percent of his passes for a school and SEC record.

He no doubt would have set more passing records in 1959 had he not had to share the time with senior Charley Britt. It still is incredible to me that *Tarkenton did not start a game in 1959!*

Of course, Tarkenton's most memorable game was against Auburn in the next to last game of 1959. He passed Georgia down the field in a late drive, then hit Bill Herron on a 13-yard fourth-down pass as Georgia won, 14-13, to nail down the SEC title. Then he tossed two TD passes as Georgia beat Missouri in the Orange Bowl on New Year's Day.

Tarkenton was even greater in the National Football League, leading the Minnesota Vikings to three Super Bowl appearances.

His Vikings coach, Bud Grant, called him "the greatest quarterback ever to play in the NFL."

He is a member of both the College and Professional Football Halls of Fame.

Florida Coach Ray Graves called him "The Golden Thread" that wove his team down the field to victory.

Georgia Bulldog poet laureate Harold M. Walker, in toasting the 1959 SEC champions at their coronation party, said:

> Here's to Athens' favorite son,
> The Peerless Pilot, Tarkenton!

Larry Rakestraw

Chapter Three

ATHLETES FROM THE MODERN ERA

1962 – Present

RAKESTRAW, THE RECORD-BREAKER

All football fans realize how tough it is to beat a good team on the road—in their own backyard—and no team is tougher to beat on its home field than Clemson in Death Valley. This story is about a rifle-armed quarterback who led Georgia to a sensational 24-16 victory over the Tigers in Death Valley in 1962.

His name was Larry Rakestraw, out of West Fulton in Atlanta, and he could toss "the bomb" about as well as any passer who ever wore the Red and Black.

The Clemson scouts should have prepared their Tigers for Rakestraw because the week before he had thrown a 69-yard TD pass to earn Georgia a 7-7 tie against South Carolina at Columbia, hitting fellow Atlantan big Mickey Babb on the play.

That feat notwithstanding, on his very first offensive play from scrimmage against Clemson, Rakestraw passed to fullback Frank Lankewicz on a 77-yard haymaker, and then he came back in the second quarter to hit speedy halfback Don Porterfield on a 74-yard scoring pitch.

But that performance was far from Rakestraw's best, which came the next year (his senior season) when he wrecked the record-book and the Miami Hurricane one hot night in the Orange Bowl. On this memorable occasion Rakestraw hooked up with Miami's All-America quarterback, George Mira, in the most torrid quarterback passing duel in American collegiate football history. Mira himself broke his own passing record with 25 of 44 for 342 yards, but Rakestraw was 25 of 38 for 407 yards (still the Georgia record) and eight of them were to end Pat Hodgson, two for TDs.

After the game, George Mira walked across the field to shake hands with Rakestraw and said to him:

"You are the greatest player I have ever seen."

Rakestraw later played several seasons with the Chicago Bears but injuries cut short his pro career.

"GENERAL GEORGE" PATTON

George Smith Patton was a great U.S. Army tank commander in World War II, the most feared opponent of the German High Command.

George Edward Patton was not a blood relative of Gen. Patton, but his "attack" tactics on the football field showed a marked resemblance to the "seek and destroy" doctrine of old "Blood and Guts." During the football seasons of 1964-65-66 Georgia's own "General George" Patton was the defensive lineman most feared by SEC ball-carriers and passers.

It was highly unusual that Georgia was able to recruit George E. Patton in 1963. One would have figured he'd go to either Ole Miss, where his older brother Houston had been a star quarterback in the 1950s, or Alabama, where another older brother Jim had played on Bear Bryant's national championship team of 1961. Furthermore, Georgia was in the doldrums, having had losing seasons in 1961 and 1962.

But he accepted a scholarship to Georgia because he felt his chances of playing quarterback would be better than at some other SEC schools. He had compiled a fine high school record at T-QB at Deshler High in Tuscumbia, Alabama. He tossed 12 TD passes his senior season, paced an upset win over the Alabama state champion, Decatur, and was a unanimous selection on the All-Tennessee Valley team.

Ironically, he wound up as fourth-string freshman quarterback at Georgia behind three very talented players: Preston Ridlehuber, Keith Sherman and Lynn Hughes. He became a disgruntled benchwarmer and began thinking that he would become the "black sheep" of his family of fine athletes.

While he didn't get to play QB for the frosh in 1963, he was given the QB job for the "B" team, the whipping boys for the varsity in scrimmages. And he did get a big kick out of leading the "B"

George Patton

team to several scrimmage victories over the freshmen that fall.

It was a fellow Alabamian, Vince Dooley of Mobile and Auburn University, who came to Patton's rescue in 1964 when he was named Georgia's new head coach. It didn't take Dooley and his assistants long to recognize that Patton had talent and should be in the lineup somewhere. So in the spring of 1964 Coach Dooley moved Patton to tackle.

"I told Coach Dooley I had rather play QB," George told me in an interview at that time. "But Georgia needed tackles, and I needed a job."

What a varsity debut Patton made at tackle in the opening game against Alabama in Tuscaloosa! On the very first defensive play from scrimmage, Patton broke through and tossed the mighty Joe Namath for a nine-yard loss. That was the first of many, many spectacular plays Patton was to make the next three years as he helped lead Georgia to three straight winning seasons, including the SEC title in 1966. He earned All-SEC honors in 1964, All-America in 1965 and 1966.

Against Auburn that soph season of 1964 Patton showed his versatility by snagging a 40-yard pass on a "tackle eligible" play to set up Georgia's only score.

As a junior in 1965, against Alabama in the opening game in Athens, Bear Bryant and the Tide were his victims. Patton intercepted a pass and raced 65 yards to score as Georgia won a sensational 18-17 game, the only loss Alabama had that year on its way to the national championship.

Perhaps his greatest game was against previously unbeaten Florida at Jacksonville when he led the rush on Heisman-award winner Steve Spurrier to pace a great Georgia victory en route to the SEC crown. Two weeks later he did the same thing to Georgia Tech in Athens, intercepting a pass that set up a score as Georgia handed Bobby Dodd's last Tech team its only loss of the season.

But the greatest thrill of George Patton's Georgia career came in the closing minutes as Georgia beat SMU in the Cotton Bowl on New Year's Day, 1967. It seems that early in Patton's career at Georgia Coach Dooley had promised George he'd let him play quarterback before he graduated. Well, he remembered in Dallas, and with Georgia leading SMU, 24-9, he put Patton in the lineup at tailback in the shotgun formation. George threw three wild passes in a row, then decided to run on fourth down and he galloped 16 yards for a first down as the game ended.

George to this day still thinks he would have been a great quarterback, and there's one thing for sure: he couldn't have been a better QB than he was a defensive tackle for the Georgia Bulldogs in 1964-65-66. And he outdid older brothers Houston and Jim, too!

BOBBY ETTER BEATS FLORIDA

Georgia fans have been a bit spoiled by our domination of the Florida series in recent years, but there was a time in the 1950s and early 1960s when Bulldog victories at Jacksonville were as scarce as a kernel of corn in a henhouse.

Georgia leads Florida in the long series, 44 to 25, and has won 13 of the last 20 games, but when Vince Dooley's first Bulldog team engaged the Gators in 1964, Georgia was trying to end a four-year losing streak. In fact, over the previous nine years only Georgia's 1959 SEC and Orange Bowl championship team had been able to whip Florida.

The hero of Georgia's 1964 upset of Florida converted a fouled-up field goal try into a thrilling touchdown run.

His name was Bobby Etter, son of a famous high school football coach in Chattanooga, Red Etter, who had another son, Gene Etter, who was a star tailback at Tennessee.

Bobby Etter was an outstanding placekicker at Georgia three years, lettered in basketball and baseball, and was a straight-A student majoring in math, which he now teaches at Sacramento State University in California. He kicked for the Atlanta Falcons two seasons and was their leading scorer both years.

Bobby won many honors as a placekicker at Georgia, including becoming the first placekicker ever to lead the SEC in scoring. His senior year, 1966, he amassed 57 points on 21 PATS and 12 field goals.

His talented toe was the margin of victory in several Georgia

Bobby Etter diving into the end zone

games, notably three field goals to beat Michigan at Ann Arbor in 1965 and a last-minute field goal to nip Mississippi State 20-17 as Georgia won the SEC crown in 1966.

But his greatest thrill by far was against Florida in Jacksonville November 7, 1964. The Gators that year were rated the strongest in their school history, and Bear Bryant at Alabama had called them the best team any of his teams had ever played. But the Bulldogs were playing over their heads this afternoon in Jacksonville and were even with the Gators 7-7 late in the fourth quarter when a drive was stopped at the Florida 5.

Coach Dooley sent Etter in to kick a short field goal, but

Georgia's holder, Barry Wilson, couldn't handle the snap from center. Etter grabbed the loose ball and lit out around left end, faking a pass as he ran that temporarily caused the Florida right sideback to drop back for the end zone pass possibility. When he did come up to tackle Etter at the goal line he was blocked by Barry Wilson (who went on to become head coach at Duke University). Etter dove over both of them for the winning score.

That play deservedly belongs in the film of Georgia's most memorable touchdown plays.

SPEED MERCHANT KENT LAWRENCE

Georgia's opening football game against Mississippi State at Jackson in 1966 was the varsity debut of probably the fastest half-back ever to wear the Red and Black of Georgia. And it also was the debut for the incomparable Larry Munson as Georgia's football play-by-play announcer.

The fleet halfback referred to was and is Kent Lawrence, a native of Clemson, South Carolina, who now is Judge Kent Lawrence of the State Court of Clarke County in Athens. Recently, in his chambers, Judge Lawrence recalled his first varsity game as a sophomore at Jackson, Mississippi.

"I really didn't expect to play much, if any, in that game," he recalled. "Senior Randy Wheeler was our regular tailback but he was injured early when tackled hard by Mississippi State's All-America linebacker, D. D. Lewis (later an all-pro with the Dallas Cowboys). So Coach Dooley put me in the lineup."

And Lawrence responded with a fine all-around performance as Georgia won, 20-17, en route to the first of Coach Dooley's six SEC championships. Lawrence went on to be the Bulldogs' No. 1 tailback three straight years.

He had an outstanding sophomore season as Georgia went 10-1, losing only to Miami in Miami by one point, 7-6. His best game was against previously unbeaten Georgia Tech in the season's finale in Athens, when he scored early on a 70-yard punt return. He also set something of a record by scoring two TDs that were nullified by penalties (a 25-yard rush and an 8-yard pass from Kirby Moore).

Perhaps his greatest game was in the Cotton Bowl against SMU New Year's Day 1967. On the very third play, he broke loose on a 74-yard touchdown run and went on to rush for 149 yards in 16 carries (a Georgia bowl record).

The late Harry Mehre, in the *Atlanta Journal*, wrote: "I have never seen a young halfback with more speed and agility than

Kent Lawrence with Vince Dooley

Lawrence." And Georgia's poet laureate, Harold M. Walker, responded with a poem entitled "Lawrence of Georgia." Its opening stanza was:

> Lawrence of Arabia was noted for his speed
> As he rode the burning desert on his trusty Arab steed;
> But now another Lawrence has come on to steal the show,
> Making his famous predecessor seem just a little slow.

Georgia track coach Speck Towns firmly believed that Lawrence was capable of making the U.S. Olympic team as a sprinter had he been able to concentrate full-time on track. In fact, in his early years at Georgia Lawrence did participate in track. He won the Florida Relays' 100-yard dash, also set a VMI Relays record of six seconds flat for the 60-yard dash, and in 1967 he almost won the NCAA Indoor 60 at Detroit. He beat famed O. J. Simpson and finished in a dead heat with Charley Greene.

Towns thought Lawrence won, but the judges gave the nod to Greene, who the next year won the Olympics 100 at Mexico City while Lawrence was leading Georgia to another SEC football crown.

BILLY PAYNE, A WINNER

The University of Georgia has had 24 father-son combinations in football. Billy Payne, a hero of two crucial victories over Ole Miss in Sanford Stadium that led to Georgia winning the SEC championship in 1966 and 1968, was part of one of them.

Billy's father, Porter Payne, was an outstanding high school fullback at old Boys' High in Atlanta, and he also played on two SEC championship teams at Georgia: 1946 and 1948. Both also made all-SEC at new positions they learned to play at Georgia: Porter at tackle and Billy at defensive end.

At Dykes High School in Atlanta Billy was an all-state T-QB, but he was switched to offensive end as a freshman at Georgia and was a very good one as a sophomore on Georgia's SEC and Cotton Bowl championship team in 1966. He was an excellent blocker

All-SEC father-son combination: Porter Payne ('48) and Billy Payne ('68)

and pass-receiver. In fact, when Georgia upset Ole Miss, 9-3, in 1966, Billy played a key part in the victory. QB Kirby Moore pulled off the same "flea-flicker" play that he had used to beat Alabama the previous year. He had Billy spot and then passed to him; Billy then lateralled to halfback Randy Wheeler, who ran 25 yards for the winning score.

Two years later, also between the hedges, the Bulldogs and Rebels met in another showdown. It was all Ole Miss in the first half with the great Archie Manning tossing a 10-yard TD pass for a 7-0 Rebel lead at intermission. But early in the second half, Billy Payne, now playing defensive end his senior year, made a tremendous leaping interception of a Manning pass to set up Georgia's first TD, and the Bulldogs went on to win, 21-7.

Billy Payne graduated in law at Georgia, and, as the president of the Atlanta Committee for the Olympic Games, played a major role in bringing the 1996 Olympic Games to his home town.

Porter Payne's son Billy has always been a winner.

GREAT SCOTT!

The exclamation "Great Scott" has been used with gusto many times by Americans for almost 150 years in tribute to the great general, Winfield Scott, hero of our army's rout of Mexico in 1847. But for the past 25 years, when Georgians say "Great Scott," they are referring to the one and only Jacob E. Scott, safetyman extraordinaire for the Georgia Bulldogs in 1967 and 1968.

Georgia has had several of the finest defensive backs ever to play American collegiate football. Charley Trippi in the 1940s was the first and Terry Hoage in the early '80s was certainly another. And there was one in between Trippi and Hoage who also made All-America and who certainly rates the "super" classification. He was the inimitable Jake Scott, who went on to make all-pro with the world champion Miami Dolphins.

I well remember Jake as a little boy playing at the Athens YMCA in preliminary games to Georgia's games in Sanford Stadium. Jake played guard for those Y teams. Coach Cobern Kelly must have had a lot of talent not to have used Jake in the backfield. As a matter of fact, his boys were good enough to win the Southern championship in their age group, and I saw most of their games since my son, Ham, was the quarterback.

Jake was moved to the backfield in high school, though, and at Georgia he was one of the main reasons the Bulldogs won the

Charley Trippi congratulating Jake Scott

1968 SEC championship. In the opening game at Knoxville against the defending SEC champions and the nation's No. 2 ranked team, the Great Jake made a sensational 90-yard punt return as Georgia tied the Vols in a 17-17 upset.

Scott turned in an All-America performance every game he played in 1968, excelling as a kickoff returner, punt returner, pass defender and tackler.

He was a gambler, too. Against Florida in Jacksonville, in a torrential rain, he took the game's first punt on the dead run instead of playing it safe, and he ran it back 56 yards to pace a 51-0 Georgia rout of the Gators.

Although Jake only played two years for Georgia, he still holds the school career record of 16 interceptions. His total of 315 yards on interception returns is also still the school record and his average return of 19.7 yards is the SEC record, too. He still holds the Georgia school record for most punt returns in one season: 35 in 1968.

He was the real "Great Scott."

"BLIND" CHARLEY WHITTEMORE

A preacher's son with poor vision and unremarkable speed became one of Georgia's best pass-catchers ever. Charley Whittemore is his name, and he was a sensational receiver in high school before he came to Athens. As a junior he led Douglas County High of Douglasville to the state title, catching

Charles Whittemore

two TD passes in the championship game.

Douglas County used the "run and shoot" offense. Charley also was a good runner, but on passing situations he would move to a receiver's position. He caught 60 passes his senior year.

Charley didn't have great speed, but he did have great hands. He had about the same speed as another immortal Georgia and NFL pass-receiver, Jimmy Orr—not at all the blazing speed of Lindsey Scott of our 1980 national championship team or like Andre Hastings of the 1991-92 Bulldogs.

I once asked Charley how he developed into such a dangerous receiver despite his less-than-bullet-speed. He gave me a most unusual answer.

"I had such poor vision," he said, "that I had to concentrate on seeing the ball a lot more than the receivers who had good vision. And when I finally put on contact lenses, the ball looked as big as a basketball, and then I had no trouble at all seeing and catching it."

Charley set a Georgia one-game receiving record with 10 catches against Kentucky in Lexington in 1970, and I'll never forget the pass he caught later the same year that helped upset Auburn in Auburn—a one-handed grab in the end zone as he fell to the turf.

Charley himself considers his best catch the one he made as a freshman that beat the Georgia Tech freshmen on Grant Field.

"It was certainly my luckiest catch," said Charley. "I lost the ball in the sun and never saw it until it hit my outstretched hands."

Charley served 13 years as an assistant Bulldog coach. Now he is administrative assistant to athletic director Vince Dooley. His son, Chad, was a star athlete at Clarke Central in Athens and now is a heavy-hitting catcher for the Georgia nine. His daughter, Amy, is in Georgia dental school at Augusta.

PAUL GILBERT'S BIG GAME

Fate has played its part in many of history's most memorable events, and it certainly did so when the Georgia football team pulled off its greatest comeback ever (at that time) one Saturday afternoon in early November, 1970.

A Homecoming crowd of 57,000—plus millions more watch-

Paul Gilbert

ing on national ABC television—was stunned as South Carolina jumped off to a 21-3 lead midway through the second quarter. Furthermore, Georgia's No. 1 quarterback, Mike Cavan, had been sidelined with an injury, joining James Ray, formerly the No. 1 QB and now No. 2, on the disabled list. Coach Dooley was down to his No. 3 quarterback, senior Paul Gilbert of Athens.

But Gilbert was not your usual No. 3 quarterback. He had

begun the 1968 season as the No. 1 quarterback, only to suffer a broken leg in the very first game, and his playing career seemed to have ended. Fate, though, gave Gilbert a chance to be No. 1 QB again this day, and he responded with one of the finest performances ever rendered in Sanford Stadium. He led Georgia to a sensational 52-34 victory.

On his first TD drive he completed long passes to Billy Brice and Charley Whittemore to the South Carolina 5, from where Robert Honeycutt ran it in. Then he passed for two points, hitting Billy Brice and closing the gap to 21-11. South Carolina retaliated and moved out front, 28-11, but Gilbert came right back on Georgia's next possession, completing four passes, then scoring on an 11-yard option run. Later he took the second half kickoff and engineered a beautiful 81-yard drive in 18 plays, scoring himself from the one. Kim Braswell's PAT closed the margin to 28-25.

South Carolina retaliated again with a field goal, stretching its lead to 31-25, but Gilbert came back with a 60-yard scoring pass to Brice, and Braswell's PAT put Georgia ahead for the first time, 32-31. It didn't last long, though. The Gamecocks hit on another field goal to go ahead, 34-32.

But fate was not going to let Paul Gilbert lose this day. He passed to Jimmy Shirer for 41 yards, then scored himself on a 10-yard run.

His work for the afternoon showed three touchdowns rushing himself and 245 yards passing—the best job ever done by a Georgia quarterback in a relief role.

"Unimpeachable" Andy Johnson

There have been 16 football players at Georgia with the name of Johnson, three of them star quarterbacks: H.F. Johnson of LaGrange, of the 1927 Dream and Wonder Team; Anderson Sydney Johnson of Athens in the early 1970s, and Wayne Johnson of Columbus from 1985-1988.

The "Unimpeachable Andy Johnson," one of the most versatile backs ever to wear the Red and Black, played nine years in the NFL for New England—not as a quarterback but as a ball-carrier and wide-receiver.

In 1969 Johnson took old Athens High (now Clarke Central) to the state championship game against powerhouse Valdosta. On the very last play of the game he passed for a touchdown and then passed for a two-point conversion to give Athens a 26-26 tie.

The next year he set a Georgia freshman total offense record of 1,078 yards in five games, and *Playboy* magazine picked him to be the sophomore-of-the-year in the nation in 1971. He lived up

Andy Johnson

to all expectations, rushing for 870 yards and scoring 13 TDs (an SEC record for a soph). He led Georgia to an 11-1 record and a Gator Bowl victory, and his greatest performance was against Georgia Tech in Atlanta when he sparked a 65-yard winning drive "against the clock" with only a minute left in the game.

Johnson led the Bulldogs to successful seasons his junior and senior seasons, too, including a thrilling 17-16 victory over Maryland in the Peach Bowl in his finale, where he scored the winning TD.

Then he played nine seasons at New England, although often handicapped with injuries. Patriots Coach Chuck Fairbanks called Andy the finest athlete he had ever coached. He was a triple-threat halfback: running, passing, and receiving.

Perhaps Andy's most memorable play as a Bulldog came against Tennessee in Knoxville in 1973. The Vols led 31-28 late in the game and faked a punt on fourth down. Georgia "smelled" it and stopped the runner, taking over at the Tennessee 26. In five running plays Georgia scored, Johnson tallying the winning TD after picking up a fumbled handoff to Gliding Glynn Harrison.

Recently I asked Andy about that famous play, and he said, "To tell the truth, the fumble was my fault. I hit Glynn's hip with the handoff and the ball fell to the tartan turf and bounced straight up into my hands. The Tennessee players didn't see the fumble and they all converged on Glynn while I slipped around left end untouched."

Even those in the press box, particularly Larry Munson in his broadcast, thought it was a beautiful fake and declared it the most perfectly executed bootleg they had ever seen.

In the meantime, the Tennessee fans were mad enough to do unto Georgia's Andy Johnson what the United States Congress had tried to do unto Tennessee's Andy Johnson back in 1868.

"GLIDING GLYNN" HARRISON

When Georgia football followers talk about the best ball-carriers who ever wore the Red and Black, there's one player they may

Glynn Harrison

not list because he didn't make All-America. But he was definitely in the class of the six Bulldog running backs who did make
the A-A selection: Bob McWhorter, Frank Sinkwich, Charley
Trippi, Herschel Walker, Tim Worley and Garrison Hearst.

His name: Glynn Harrison, who came to Georgia from
Columbia High in Decatur, Georgia, as a freshman back in 1972
and starred for the Bullpups that season when freshmen were

not eligible for the varsity.

As a sophomore in 1973 Coach Dooley had two outstanding senior backs, Jimmy Poulos (the Greek Streak) and Horace (The Horrific) King. But Coach Dooley wanted to get Harrison's speed and talent in the lineup somewhere. So he utilized him as a specialist in covering kicks and returning kicks, and occasionally he would sub for Poulos and King.

After his sophomore season, Coach Dooley called Harrison "the best we've ever had covering kicks."

But Coach Dooley had other plans for Gliding Glynn in 1974. He wanted him to be his No. 1 running back, which role he superbly filled that season and again in 1975.

Gliding Glynn made many great runs for Georgia. His first one came on a punt return as a sophomore in 1973 against Tennessee in Knoxville (42 yards). But perhaps Glynn's finest run was against Florida in 1975, a brilliant 87-yard off tackle burst for a TD that was nullified by a penalty. And Georgia Bulldogs will never forget his great run that did count two weeks later against The Enemy on Grant Field Thanksgiving Night, 1975, on national television. It was 78 yards to highlight a Bulldog triumph en route to the Cotton Bowl.

In Georgia's record book, Glynn Harrison is listed as the second-best ever in average gain per rush: 6.37 yards per carry, just behind Charley Trippi's 6.42.

Pretty good for a former kick-covering and kick-return specialist!

GEORGIA'S "GREATEST" QUARTERBACK

Georgia has had a dozen All-SEC quarterbacks, and by far the "greatest" was the strapping south Georgian from Moultrie who led the Bulldogs to the conference crown in 1976. He stood 6-2 and tipped the scales at 220 pounds.

Seriously, Ray Goff was a truly *great* player in more ways than size. He was voted the SEC's player-of-the-year his senior season, an honor accorded only six other Bulldogs in the 60-year history of the league: Frank Sinkwich, 1942; Charley Trippi, 1946;

Johnny Rauch, 1948; Jake Scott, 1968; Willie McClendon, 1978; and Herschel Walker, 1980-81-82.

"The fans probably didn't realize how big Ray was for a quarterback because we had such a gigantic line (All-Americans Moonpie Wilson, Cowboy Parrish, Randy Johnson and George Collins) that when we lined up in the huddle he didn't look any bigger than Kirby Moore or Buck Belue standing next to those giants," pointed out Coach Dooley.

In 1974 Goff was the No. 2 QB behind fellow soph Matt Robinson, the better passer of the two and a future NFL starter; Georgia went 6-6, losing their last three games against Auburn, Georgia Tech and Miami (Ohio) in the Tangerine Bowl. But in

Current Top Dawg Ray Goff

spring practice of 1975 Goff won the starting QB role, and that fall he almost led Georgia to the SEC title. Our only league loss was to Ole Miss at Oxford, and I always will believe that we would have beaten the Rebels that day had Goff not gone down with an elbow injury in the first quarter with Georgia ahead, 7-0, on the strength of a 17-yard TD run by Goff.

However, Rugged Ray never missed another game during his Georgia career, and he led Georgia to a 9-2 season and to the Cotton Bowl in 1975. The next year he led the Bulldogs to a great 10-1 season, the SEC crown, and to the Sugar Bowl where Pittsburgh proved too strong in a battle for the national championship.

Some of Goff's finest performances came during his sensational senior season in 1976, starting with a 73-yard TD run vs. Clemson in Death Valley, followed by a 70-yard run and a 75-yard pass to Gene Washington for TDs at Ole Miss, a 63-yard TD jaunt vs. Vandy the next week, and a stupendous day as Georgia rallied from a 27-13 halftime deficit against Florida to win 41-27. Goff was 5 of 5 passing for 37 yards and two TDs and had 184 yards rushing and three TDs, which earned him player-of-the-week honors in the nation.

His most memorable play for me, though, came against Vanderbilt in Nashville his junior year. He was the key man in the execution of the slickest trick play I have ever seen—the famous "shoe-string" play.

It took place early in the second quarter with Georgia leading, 7-3. In watching Vandy films, Georgia offensive line coach Jimmy Vickers had noticed that the Commodores held hands while in their defensive huddle, and it was Jimmy who suggested to Coach Dooley the possibility of working the shoe-string while the Vandy players were in their prolonged huddle.

Goff set it up by running a sweep around right end out of bounds so the ball would be placed on the extreme right hash mark. Then on the next play, as Vandy players huddled, Ray went up to the ball, got down on one knee and pretended to tie his shoe strings. In the meantime, the Georgia players quickly lined up (all the linemen to the left of the ball, three backs in the backfield). Simultaneously, Goff picked up the ball and shovel-passed it to speed merchant Gene Washington, who skirted left end 36 yards to goal with a fleet of blockers. The Vandy players finally broke their huddle and began chasing Washington as he crossed the goal line.

I also recall that Coach Dooley had informed the officials before the game that Georgia planned to use the shoe-string play. He didn't want the officials to think it was an illegal play, and Coach Dooley's action was really the smartest maneuver of the day.

REX ROBINSON

Georgia has had more than its share of superb placekickers, headed by two who made All-America not only once but twice: Rex Robinson of Marietta and Kevin Butler of Stone Mountain.

Noble Rexford Robinson was the police chief's son whose talented toe won 10 games during his Bulldog career—more than any other Georgia kicker in history.

The South Carolina Gamecocks painfully remember him. Rex kicked two field goals to beat them in Columbia, 15-13, in 1977, his freshman year, and again three years later he booted a pair of field goals to win a very important game, 13-10, in Athens as Georgia went on to an undefeated season and the national championship.

But Rex is best remembered for a field goal late in the season of 1978 at Lexington, Kentucky. It capped a sensational Georgia comeback. Down 16-0 in the third quarter, the Dogs pulled up to 14-16 and were at the Wildcats' 12 with only three seconds left in the game. That's when Coach Dooley, on the sidelines, yelled to his big right tackle Tim Morrison: "What are you doing here?" To which Morrison replied: "I'm praying that Rex will make that field goal, Coach." To which Coach Dooley exclaimed: "My God; you're supposed to be in there right now blocking for Robinson. We only have 10 men on the field." Fortunately, Coach Curci of Kentucky called a timeout to put some added pressure on Robinson, which enabled Morrison to rush back on the field.

And when Rex kicked that 29-yard field goal Georgia's immor-

Rex Robinson

tal Larry Munson uttered his famous "Yeah! Yeah! Yeah! It's good!" as Georgia won 16-15.

Yes, Rex Robinson did pretty good for a placekicker who missed his first PAT try against Oregon State, then never missed again during a four-year career: 101 consecutive PATS, then the SEC record and still the Georgia mark.

"THE GOAL-LINE STALKER"

In Georgia's annual football brochure, there is one full page devoted to all the NCAA, SEC and Georgia school records set by Herschel Walker, "the goal-line stalker."

And I well remember his setting all those incredible marks. But here are two other things I also remember about Herschel during his three glorious years in Athens that beautifully portray his character.

First, he made satisfactory school marks because he attended class regularly and religiously kept up with his assignments. My wife, Rosemary, taught Herschel freshman English and likes to tell this story about him. She had scheduled the usual Friday morning theme the day before the big game with Florida in Jacksonville. So some of the students asked that the theme be rescheduled because they wanted a long weekend in Jacksonville for the big game. Rosemary polled each student to see how many were going to Jacksonville and would be absent Friday morning. Everyone raised his hand but one student: Herschel Walker. He said the team was not leaving until Friday afternoon and that he would attend class that morning.

Herschel was my wife's only student that quarter who never cut a single class. However, he was not able to be present for the final examination as he was on national television on the Bob Hope All-America show. The University allowed him to schedule a make-up exam later.

In the spring following Herschel's last season at Georgia I invited him to play in the Celebrity Doubles event during the annual Collegiate Tennis Hall of Fame ceremonies honoring newly elected members, which were held at our Henry Field Stadium during the NCAAs. Herschel said he'd be glad to take part, but I would have to guarantee him one thing.

"I never have played much tennis and I don't want to embarrass myself out there," said Herschel. "You'll have to teach me to play doubles."

Herschel worked out on our tennis courts almost every day for a month with Manuel Diaz and I taking turns coaching him. Being a super athlete, Herschel caught on fast; and he did a superb job in the Celebrity Doubles, teaming with former

Wimbledon doubles champion Dennis Ralston, the SMU coach.

Prior to that episode I also recall that one day, when I arrived at our tennis courts, I was shocked to see black marks all over the No. 1 court, caused by someone playing with "jogging" shoes instead of tennis shoes. Immediately I asked our groundskeeper, James Payne (father of Georgia All-America tackle Jimmy Payne), "Who made those black marks on the court?"

James replied: "The only people who have played on the No. 1 court were two football players. Herschel Walker was one of them."

"Oh," I said. "Well, I'm sure Herschel didn't mean any harm." That's when I got the idea of asking Herschel to play in the Celebrity Doubles—and I also gave him a pair of tennis shoes to replace those "damned" jogging shoes.

THOM WHITE

"The Service-Line Stalker"

EVERY WHICH WAY BELUE

Benjamin Franklin (Buck) Belue, the pride of Valdosta, never received sufficient credit for the big part he played in piloting Georgia to the national football championship in 1980. Most of the credit deservedly was given to the player Buck so often handed the ball to: Herschel Walker.

But Buck Belue was a great player himself, the sparkplug of many sensational plays. And only one player in Red and Black history ever threw more TD passes than Buck. Johnny Rauch, as a four-year regular QB in 1945-6-7-8, tossed 33 Td passes, Buck 32 in only three years as the regular QB (1979-80-81).

Furthermore, in Buck's senior year (1981) he almost led Georgia to a second straight national championship. A lot of people have forgotten that Georgia led Pitt, 20-17, after Buck hit Clarence Kay on a 6-yard TD pass late in the fourth quarter in the Sugar Bowl and would have repeated as national champion had not the Panthers' Dan Marino connected on a fourth-down 33-yard TD pass with only 35 seconds remaining in the game. (Does anyone know what became of Marino?)

As a freshman in 1978, when he was a substitute QB behind Jeff Pyburn, Buck was the hero of Georgia's greatest comeback win in history against Georgia Tech in Sanford Stadium.

Georgia alumnus Dewey Benefield (now the Jones family's right hand in running Sea Island) put that feat into poetry, his opening stanza being:

> Neath a grim, gray December sky
> The Bulldogs found a hero
> When Buck Belue came on the field
> With the score 20-zero.

That was late in the second quarter. And Buck didn't look like a freshman as he brilliantly directed a 55-yard scoring drive. But his best was yet to come. With Tech leading, 28-21 and 5:52 left on the clock, Dooley gave his freshman QB a chance to win the game. He responded by moving the Dogs 84 yards to goal, both running and passing like an All-American. It was fourth down and three when he rolled to his right, jumped and hit Amp

Buck Belue

Arnold on a 42-yard TD play to make the score 27-28. Coach Dooley decided to play to win instead of tie. And Buck again came through on the two-point try. He faked a handoff to full-back Matt Simon, then pitched out, again to Arnold who pranced across the goal line for a stunning 29-28 Bulldog victory.

Buck never lost to Florida or Tech during his entire career as a Bulldog.

Against the Gators in Jacksonville, to the great pleasure of his fellow south Georgians who literally live for this classic, Buck always was at his best. As a sophomore in 1979 he threw three TD passes to beat Florida 33-10. The next year was his most memorable performance against the Gators, when he and Lindsay Scott hooked up on one of football's most thrilling TD passes ever. Florida was leading 21-20 with only 1:35 left. The Bulldogs were on their eight yard line, third down and 10, when Buck rolled to his right and hit Lindsey up the middle. Scott hauled it in and raced 93 yards to goal.

Two months later, in New Orleans when Georgia beat Notre Dame for the national title, Buck was at the controls when Georgia ran out the clock, leading 17-10 with 2:56 left. Buck clicked off three vital first downs, one of which he made running himself and another on a fine pass to Amp Arnold.

Buck had a great senior year in 1981, tossing 12 TD passes, two of them to Walker as the Bulldogs trimmed Florida, 26-21, in a key victory en route to the SEC crown. He tossed a pair of TD passes the next week against Auburn as Georgia clinched the title, and in a play that was one of the sweetest ever to Georgia fans, he threw a TD pass to Lindsay Scott on the game's very first play against The Enemy in Grant Field as he directed a great 44-7 triumph in his swan song versus the Yellow Jackets.

Don't ever forget Benjamin Franklin (Buck) Belue when you name Georgia's greatest quarterbacks.

The Butler Did It

The greatest placekicker in Georgia and Southeastern Conference history was lucky to get a scholarship to college. That's right. When Kevin Butler began his football career at Redan High in Stone Mountain, Georgia, he was not good enough to start as a defensive back, which caused him to contemplate quitting the game. But his dad suggested he take up placekicking since he had been a very good soccer player, and he was an immediate success. He kicked six field goals of 50 yards or better his junior year as Redan won the state title, and he had college scouts from all over the country writing him letters, including Vince Dooley of Georgia.

But misfortune hit him his senior year of 1980. In his first game, he tore ligaments in a knee and was out for the season. All the coaches—except one—who were hot after him in 1979 lost interest in a kicker with a bad leg. His injured knee required surgery, and when he woke up in the hospital after the operation the coach who had stuck with him was on the telephone. "We still want you at Georgia," Vince Dooley told a jubilant Butler.

It was a gamble for Dooley that paid off with the jackpot. What a fabulous four-year career Butler had with the Bulldogs:

In 1981 he tied the NCAA record for field goals by a freshman (19); he set the Georgia and SEC record for most points scored kicking in a season (94).

In 1982 he set a school record with a 59-yard field goal vs. Ole Miss, and his 44-yarder with only 1:11 left on the clock beat BYU.

In 1983 he began the season by tying Clemson 16-16, with a 31-yard FG with only 38 seconds left, and his PAT in the fourth quarter edged Florida, 10-9, at Jacksonville. He also nipped Texas, 10-9, with a PAT late in the game in Cotton Bowl New Year's Day, 1984, which knocked the Longhorns out of the national championship.

Some of his greatest kicks came his senior season in 1984. He booted a tremendous 60-yard FG to clip Clemson with only 11 seconds left on the clock, 26-23, tying the SEC mark. Amazingly, he hit on five of six FG attempts over 50 yards: 51 and 60 vs. Clemson, 51 vs. Vanderbilt, 50 and 57 vs. Georgia Tech.

Butler still holds the SEC records for career FGs (77), most FGs over 50 yards (11), and most points scored by a kicker (353).

Plus, he was extremely valuable as a kickoff man, over 70 percent of his kickoffs going so deep into the end zone that they were not returned.

Butler not only is Georgia's and the SEC's all-time leading scorer via placekicking, he also holds that distinction with the Chicago Bears: 722 points in eight seasons (1985-92). Other Chicago records held by Butler include: most career FGs (153); most points in a season (144 in 1985 as the Bears won the NFL); most FGs in a season (31 in 1985); most consecutive FGs made

(24 in 1988-89); most FGs over 50 yards (8); best FG percentage for career (72.5).

United States Senator Strom Thurmond of South Carolina saw Kevin kick against the Gamecocks in Columbia and quipped: "He must be the most popular Butler in Georgia since Rhett."

Jacksonville Times-Union sportswriter Greg Larson penned: "Kevin Butler has only one foot. The other is a launching pad."

Perhaps Butler's greatest honor came when he was added to the famed Confederate Memorial that is sculpted on the sheer granite side of Stone Mountain not far from his home. That is, *Atlanta Constitution* cartoonist, Scrawls, did an editorial page cartoon that had Butler, in his Georgia football uniform, astride a horse right next to General Robert E. Lee and General Stonewall Jackson.

Kevin Butler and other notable Southerners

Pop Warner

Chapter Four

THE COACHES

"THE GREAT ORIGINATOR"

Glenn S. (Pop) Warner, known as "The Great Originator," began his illustrious football coaching career at Georgia in 1895 when he was fresh out of Cornell where he had starred as a player. He had an undefeated season his second and final year at Georgia (4-0) and in his last game Georgia beat Auburn, 12-6, in a famous battle between two undefeated teams at old Brisbine Park in Atlanta before over 8,000 fans, said to have been the largest crowd ever to see a football game south of Philadelphia.

In this victory over Auburn, Warner used three so-called "trick" plays:

> (1) reverses, which called for passing behind the line of scrimmage (lateral passes).

> (2) the first huddle ever seen on a football field. Following the huddle Georgia would get off its play without a signal, catching the Auburn players flat-footed.

> (3) the short kickoff. That is, when all the Auburn players would form together at their goal line (awaiting the regular kickoff) to get ready to use the "flying wedge," Warner surprised them with the so-called short kickoff, now known as the onside kick.

Some 54 years later in 1950, following Pop's great career as coach of the Carlisle Indians (and Jim Thorpe), Pittsburgh and Stanford, I looked him up when I was in San Francisco doing advance publicity for our game with St. Mary's. He was living in

,y Palo Alto. I asked him to be Coach Butts' guest on the ,orgia bench for the game against St. Mary's in old Kezar Stadium. He accepted with tears in his eyes. He was just a shell of his former great physique: bent, stooped, walking with a cane and suffering all over with arthritis.

I asked Coach Butts to introduce Pop to the Georgia team in the dressing room before the game, which Coach Butts did, saying: "Boys, I want you to meet the greatest football coach of all time, Pop Warner." Pop then briefly recalled his days in Athens and then added, "You boys don't have to worry about this St. Mary's team. You will have no trouble with them. They are just like a high school team compared to you."

Well, Coach Butts was fit to be tied and almost foaming at the mouth. This was not the kind of "pep talk" a coach gives his team before a big game, and to make matters much worse, a few minutes later St. Mary's big John Henry Johnson ran back the opening kickoff 100 yards.

(By the way, this was the same John Henry Johnson who went on to become all-pro and, who, in one of the dirtiest plays in the history of football, later ended the career of the incomparable Charley Trippi with an elbow between the eyes that shattered Trippi's nose and cracked his skull. The operation on his nose, however, made him a damned sight better looking than he used to be.)

Georgia was lucky to tie St. Mary's that night, and I was lucky Coach Butts didn't make me return to Athens by bus instead of with the team by plane.

THE ONE AND ONLY JONESEY

Walter T. Forbes, Sr., brought Clarence Jones to Athens in 1912 as physical director of the YMCA. He carried on the great program that "W. T." began, and the Athens Y developed the finest program for boys in the United States.

Jonesey originated the Northeast Georgia basketball tournament, which became the biggest basketball tournament in the nation, attracting over 100 high school teams. There would be three games going on at the same time in old Woodruff Hall. Of

Clarence "Jonesey" Jones (right) with Fred Birchmore

course, basketball was a YMCA game, having been invented at the Springfield (Massachusetts) Y by James Naismith.

He also made Athens the swimming capital of the state. He formed Georgia's first swimming team in 1926, and his first captain was Walter T. Forbes, Jr. Walter was followed by nine other Athens boys as Bulldog captains who were his proteges at the Athens Y: John Hodgson, Fred Hodgson, Morton Hodgson Jr., Howell Erwin, John Ashford, Goodloe Erwin, Jimmy Hudson and Theyx Stewart.

A foot infection caused Jonesey the loss of a leg, but it did not slow him up. He was the Georgia football team's trainer under Harry Mehre and Wallace Butts for a few years during World War II when he came out of retirement and was also the boxing and swimming coach for a long time.

He knew a great deal about boxing, having learned much about the ring from his close friend in Illinois, the famous "uncrowned" champion, Packy McFarland. I remember his stories about Packy as I listened in the back seat of his old Dodge on swimming trips. He knew Red Grange, the Galloping Ghost, when he was a boy and Jonesey was the Athletic Director at Wheaton College, where he coached Red's older brother Ross in basketball.

Jonesey allowed "no cursing" on his teams, and some of the roughest characters ever to wear the Red and Black football uniform were in awe of him and dared not break his rule in his presence. They knew how strong he was. They had heard the story about how he had "punished" an offender—the biggest, strongest player on the team—by grabbing him by the shoulder with one hand and applying so much pressure that the fellow fell to the floor begging for mercy, which Jonesey quickly granted when he promised never to curse again.

The players loved Jonesey. He was always in good humor and called them "sonnyboy" or "knocker" in that high-pitched Welsh voice of his. Many of his players would attend church just to hear him sing in the choir at the First Methodist Church.

It was said that Jonesey developed that super-human strength in his arms and shoulders during his years as a circus performer before he came to Athens. He was the anchorman of an act that had several Japanese performing atop a bamboo pole, which he held.

One of the most famous stories about Jonesey had him knocking out Georgia's toughest player in the mid-1930s, a rough hombre who later played professional football. This player was on a drunken spree, tearing up things in a hotel room, when Jonesey, in his unique style and high voice, told him, "Now sonnyboy, you had better behave." He didn't, so Jonesey knocked him out with one punch in order to keep the police from being called.

Years later, when Coach Butts heard the story (it wasn't about one of his own players), he visited Jonesey and asked him to give him the real low-down. Jonesey just smiled and said modestly, "Well, Wally, I did have to give the fellow a little tap on the jaw."

HARRY MEHRE, ONE OF ROCKNE'S MOST FAMOUS DISCIPLES

Remembering Coach Harry Mehre brings back memories of some of the most glorious chapters in the history of Georgia football.

Coach Mehre spent 14 years of his life in Athens. He married an Athens girl, Hallie Kilpatrick, the sister of Georgia halfback Martin (Buster) Kilpatrick, who went on to head one of the south's most prominent law firms in Atlanta.

George (Kid) Woodruff brought Harry Mehre to Athens in 1924 as his line coach, specifically to install Knute Rockne's famed Notre Dame box formation offense. Mehre had been a star center for Rockne with the Irish. The goal was to make Georgia a national power. It took five years of hard work, but in 1927 Georgia's famous Dream and Wonder team, led by a pair of All-America ends (Chick Shiver and Tom Nash), stunned the nation by upsetting mighty Yale in New Haven in the second game of the season, 14-10. Then the Bulldogs annihilated seven consecutive foes, including a 20-6 victory over Alabama (even then the scourge of Southern football, boasting five straight wins over Georgia). The experts ranked Georgia No. 1 in the land, and a Rose Bowl bid was to be given Georgia as soon as it beat Georgia Tech in the finale in Atlanta. But Tech had a great team, too, and upset the Bulldogs on a mud-soaked Grant Field, 12-0.

Kid Woodruff retired as coach after that 1927 season (it had been his plan all along to stay in Athens only until Georgia was a national power; he coached the team as a hobby, being a millionaire businessman in Columbus) and was succeeded by his first assistant Harry Mehre. Harry kept Georgia in the national limelight. In 1929 his young Bulldogs again stunned Yale in the dedication of the South's finest football arena at that time, Sanford Stadium. This game had the most promotion ever given an athletic event in the South. Governors of all the Southern states were on hand. Old Athens rocked with big social events for days

Harry Mehre

in advance. President S. V. Sanford and Athletic Director Herman Stegeman had talked Yale into leaving the East for the first time in its history. After all, Yale had a close bond with Georgia, the university's first presidents being Yale grads.

When the Yale contingent finally arrived by train, practically all Athens and the Georgia student body—plus a multitude of dignitaries—were there to greet them. I was only eight years old, but I was there, and the main thing I remember was the Yale band. They could really strut. They marched all the way up College Avenue until they reached the "reviewing stand" by City Hall (their headquarters was the old Georgian Hotel just around the corner). Though Athens had the red carpet out for its guests, many Athenians still remembered too vividly the day Marse Robert surrendered to Grant. But when the Yale band broke into "Dixie" as it smartly pranced by the "reviewing stand," they won the hearts of all in Athens, and you never heard such a cheer go up. It sent goose pimples up and down my body.

A great gangling young athlete from Macon led Georgia to a 15-0 victory over Yale. His name was Vernon (Catfish) Smith and he scored all 15 points himself. He went on to make All-America end in 1931 when he and the other Flaming Sophs of 1929 (now seniors) almost put Georgia in the Rose Bowl (before losing a heartbreaker to a powerful Tulane team late in the season in Athens).

Catfish recently recalled one of the stories Harry always told at his after-dinner speeches. It was Harry's debut as a varsity play-er at Notre Dame—the regular Irish center was injured. They were playing Army in the rain and were backed up to their own goal line, fourth down. Rockne called Mehre over and told him: "Get in there, and if you make a bad snap I will kill you." Harry ran onto the field and went straight up to Slip Madigan, the guard who used to be a center, saying, "Slip, Rock wants you to make the snap." Harry exchanged positions with Madigan who made a fine snap, and when Mehre came off the field, Rockne hollered: "Great snap, Mehre. You are starting next week." At the same time, Madigan said to Mehre: "My silence will cost you 10 dollars"—a lot of money in those days.

Catfish also recalled the classical story about Coach Stegeman (one of the greatest teasers and jokers ever) when Georgia returned to the Atlanta train station after suffering a terrible defeat by national champion Southern Cal in Los Angeles. Harry said to Stege, "Loan me a nickel. I want to call a friend." Stege retorted, "Here, take a dime and call all your friends."

My favorite Coach Mehre story was about the Southern official at a Georgia-NYU game in Yankee Stadium who was tired of the "home-cooking" by the Yankee officials. NYU was about to overtake the Bulldogs late in the game but fumbled. There was a big pile-up. The Southern official dove in and came up with the ball, exclaiming "Our ball! First and ten."

Harry Mehre led Georgia to many great moments in football. One of them was in New York late in the 1936 season against mighty Fordham, unbeaten and headed for the Rose Bowl. Jim Crowley, one of the Four Horsemen at Notre Dame who had begun his coaching career at Georgia with Harry in the mid-1920s, was head coach at Fordham. His line coach was a young man named Frank Leahy and one of his star guards was named Vince Lombardi. Georgia knocked Fordham out of the Rose Bowl by tying them 7-7.

Harry left Georgia after the 1937 campaign. He had excellent teams at Georgia, but Alabama, LSU and Tennessee took turns winning the SEC title and the Georgia alumni were disgruntled. So he went to Ole Miss and he developed two of the greatest teams ever to play in the South in 1940 and 1941. He returned to the stadium he built in 1940 (Frank Sinkwich's sophomore year) and trounced Georgia, 28-14, proving that old line, "a champion can come back."

But Harry Mehre's happiest days were spent making Georgia a national power in football and, in his later years, coming back to Athens town and writing for the *Atlanta Journal* about his beloved Bulldogs.

HOWELL HOLLIS

Coach Howell Tharpe Hollis was inducted into the State of Georgia Athletic Hall of Fame in 1973 because his Georgia golf teams compiled the most successful record in the history of the

Howell Hollis

Southeastern Conference (13 team championships). But he also was worthy of being selected because of his outstanding achievements as a coach in both high school and college football, and as a college business manager of athletics during hard times.

He molded championship high school football teams at Greensboro and Athens. At Newnan High, incidentally, he met his future wife, the former Margaret McRitchie, who was one of his students.

He turned out several undefeated Georgia freshman teams: 1937-41 and 1946-47, his most famous team being the 1939 "Point-A-Minute" Bullpups (led by Frankie Sinkwich).

During World War II, Coach Hollis served as a lieutenant commander in the Navy and was stationed at Iowa City Pre-Flight school with Jim Tatum (later to become a Hall of Fame coach). They became close personal friends, and when the war ended Tatum became head coach at Oklahoma and immediately offered the backfield job to Hollis. Coach Hollis thought over Tatum's offer and decided he belonged back in Athens. So he returned to Georgia as Wallace Butts' freshman coach. Tatum gave the job to another young officer who had served with him at Iowa City, Bud Wilkinson, who went on to succeed Tatum and became a Hall of Fame coach himself. Tatum moved on to Maryland and made the Terps a national power.

Charlie Trippi, who played left halfback on Hollis' unbeaten Georgia freshman team of 1940, says "Coach Hollis was strictly business as a football coach. His teams were sound and made few mistakes on offense or defense. They were always well prepared in every phase of the game."

Coach Hollis's longtime friend and fellow coach, Bill Hartman, recalls: "He also was the ideal man to be Georgia's business manager of athletics when we were financially in the red. He looked after that money, what there was, like it was his own. I remember at the end of the 1941 season, Coach Butts sent three of us (myself, J. B. Whitworth and Hollis) to Miami to make arrangements for our trip to play TCU in the Orange Bowl. He gave Hollis $100 to take care of all the expenses—travel, hotel, meals— and Hollis returned to Athens with several dollars to spare."

Dr. Jimmy Allen, retired Athens dentist, was another of Coach Hollis' longtime friends.

"Howell was like a big brother to me when my wife and I moved from Birmingham to Athens," he recalled. "We lived close to each other on Milledge Circle and played golf together over 40 years, and together we recruited my younger brother Heyward (captain of Georgia's 1941 Orange Bowl champions) to play at Georgia.

"Golf, of course, was Howell's first love. He coached the Georgia team as a hobby and made Georgia a national power, and he was a very good 'country' golfer himself. He won the Athens Country Club championship in competition with some of the best players we ever had. I've never known a greater competitor on the golf course, and I have never known a golfer to look longer for a ball lost in the rough. He would search for it well over the official time limit of five minutes. One day, Tommy Gerdine secretly brought along his cooking timer, and when Hollis lost his ball in the rough, Tommy pulled out the cooking timer and when the buzzer sounded at five minutes, we all yelled, "Time is up.' "

I learned much from Coach Hollis myself. He taught a math course at old Athens High when I was there and he also was my tennis coach at Georgia in 1941. And we used to play a lot of doubles together against the late Hugh Hodgson (for years head of Georgia's music department) and the late Joe Wickliffe of the C&S Bank.

One of Coach Hollis' greatest achievements was making an "A" student out of me in math. He was a stern disciplinarian and stood for no nonsense among the students. I was afraid not to pay attention to him.

There have been quite a few high school football coaches and assistant college coaches who, had they ever had the opportunity, would have been great head coaches on the college level. Howell T. Hollis was one of them.

BILL HARTMAN'S GREATEST RUN

The Scene: the late 1930s when Wallace Butts had just been named head football coach at Georgia and was in the process of assembling a group of players (Sinkwich, Trippi, etc.) and coaches who would win Georgia's first SEC football title (1942) and also beat UCLA in the Rose Bowl. Bill Hartman, who played for Butts in prep school at Georgia Military College in Milledgeville and who had captained Georgia's 1937 team, had given up a promising professional football career with Washington to become Butts' backfield coach.

One summer day during this time Bobby Troutman (later a

distinguished Atlanta attorney), brought to Athens a hideous, phosphorous-covered mask, that would light up in the dark and looked like the devil. Troutman had picked it up in Boston while visiting his roommate at Harvard, our late commander-in-chief, John Fitzgerald Kennedy.

Troutman showed this mask to his good friend and Chi Phi fraternity brother when he was at Georgia, the Bulldogs' young backfield coach, Bill Hartman.

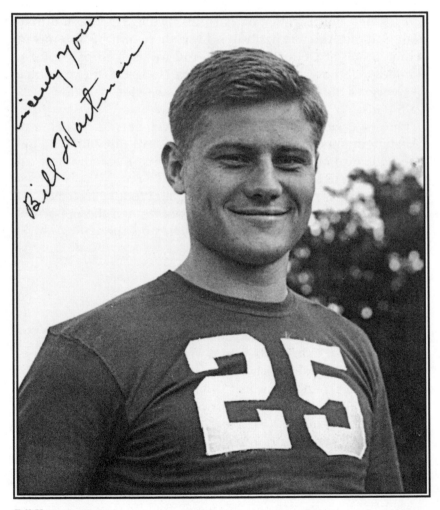

Bill Hartman

Bill was impressed. "This is a terrific mask," he said. "I'm going to put it on and go down to the boiler room in the basement of Memorial Hall and scare the daylights out of Arthur." Arthur was the old janitor who for years "looked after" Memorial Hall.

However, the fun-loving coach and devious "Speck" Towns, Georgia's young track coach, overheard Coach Hartman and immediately slipped away and ran down to the boiler room and tipped Arthur. He also gave Arthur his track starter's pistol— loaded with blank cartridges.

In the meantime, Coach Hartman put on his mask, and a goodly number of fellow assistant coaches and hangers-on followed Hartman toward the boiler room. Just before Coach Hartman went into the room he turned to his followers and whispered, "You all had better stand back from this door because Arthur is really going to be running when I scare him out of there."

Then Bill went into the dark boiler room and crept up behind Arthur. "Arthur," he intoned, "I'm the devil and I've come to fetch you." With that, Arthur pulled out the pistol and opened fire. Coach Hartman frantically ran to the door and, unable to find the door knob in the dark, he banged his shoulder against the door until he knocked it down. He came roaring past his followers out in the hall with Arthur pursuing right behind him. It was without a doubt Bill Hartman's greatest run.

———— ■ ————

When I think of William Coleman Hartman, Jr., I think of a solid citizen: the Rock of Gibraltar, the Goodyear Blimp, a fellow to play Santa Claus without needing any pillows.

The first time I laid eyes on him (and his lifelong friend, Walter Troutman), was back in the summer of 1934 when they were cabin leaders at the Athens Y Camp up above Tallulah Falls. Almost every night they committed a cardinal sin; that is, they would slip out and walk over the mountain to visit their rich Atlanta girlfriends on Lake Rabun, which was a "belt-line" offense if caught. I'd tell on them now, but Camp Director Bobby Hoods is dead, and I don't know anybody else who could make them run through the "belt line."

Bill was a young high school quarterback in Madison, a great halfback under Wallace Butts at GMC, and a versatile college player under Harry Mehre at Georgia (left halfback, fullback, quarterback, linebacker, captain of the team, All-SEC and All-America).

Among "Billy Belly's" remarkable athletic feats are the longest punt ever made in Sanford Stadium (at that time)—82 yards on the fly against Tulane in 1937—and a 93-yard kickoff return that tied Tech at Grant Field in 1937.

Bill is also remembered as the young understudy for the legendary Sammy Baugh at tailback for the Washington Redskins in 1938, who played the whole season for the injured Baugh and did a superb job, once completing 13 straight passes.

He became the first assistant coach hired by Wallace Butts at Georgia in 1939, a young man who was the greatest player Butts ever coached in 10 years of prep ball. I like to think of Frankie Sinkwich and Charley Trippi and their young backfield coach during Georgia's first Golden Years of winning conference championships and bowl games, and of how this young coach taught Sinkwich and Trippi the finer points of the game.

Bill was the man rightfully selected to succeed the immortal George (Kid) Woodruff as chairman of the Georgia Student Educational Fund, the backbone of Georgia's athletic scholarship fund, a position of trust he has held for three decades.

Later he came out of retirement (at Coach Dooley's request) to coach Georgia kickers, and, luckily he was so rich he could do it without pay.

Bill Hartman, to sum it all up, has done more for his alma mater than any other person I know.

NATIVE SON WALLACE BUTTS

It was the middle of the 1939 football season on a cold, rainy day in New York's legendary Yankee Stadium. Coach Wallace Butts' first Georgia football team was playing New York University. High up in the press box, Robert Kelley, esteemed sports editor of the *New York Times*, came over to a group of Georgia sportswriters. He asked me, then sports editor of the *Athens Banner-Herald*, "What nationality is Coach Butts? He looks like a blond Dutchman to me." I replied, "I swear, I just don't know what nationality Coach Butts is."

Then the old gentleman sitting to my right snapped out, "Why, he's a Georgia Cracker—that's what nationality he is."

It was the voice of another real Georgia Cracker, the late Edwin Camp, brilliant editorialist for the *Atlanta Journal* who wrote sports as a hobby under the pen name of Ole Timer.

James Wallace Butts, indeed, was a full-blooded Georgia Cracker—I later learned of Scotch-Irish-English stock—and he was a direct descendant of Captain Samuel Butts, one of Georgia's earliest settlers, for whom Butts County, Georgia, is named. Captain Butts was killed leading a charge of Georgia Militia against Creek Indians in the Battle of Chalibbe January 27, 1814.

Coach Butts was born in Milledgeville, in the very heart of

August company: (l-r) Herman Talmadge, Wallace Butts, Dan Magill

Georgia, February 7, 1905. As a boy he worked in the brickyards and loaded wagons for his dad, who was a draymaster. That's how he developed those tremendously muscled forearms. What a weightlifter he could have been! But he grew up before weightlifting became an official sports competition. He also coached before blacks played football at Georgia, and it is a shame he did. What rapport he always had with the blacks. How he loved them and they loved him, too, and what stories he could tell about his many days as a boy working with them in the brickyards of Milledgeville.

One of Coach Butts' favorite characters was the late Clegg Stark, Georgia's famous water boy. Coach Butts also was one of Clegg's favorite characters, and many were the stories they told on each other. Coach Butts particularly loved the one about the time some Georgia alumni bought a house for Clegg and gave him the keys to it, whereupon Clegg said, "I appreciate all this, Coach Butts, but whose gonna pay the taxes?"

Coach Butts was a master raconteur. He often referred to his beloved wife, Winnie, as "Miz Butts," and one of his best-known stories was about the time Winnie told him he was working too hard and needed to relax and think about things besides football and try to improve his mind. She took him to a nightclub where there was a great floorshow with a lot of pretty follies-girls. Coach Butts would comment, "I don't know whether Miz Butts' taking me to this club improved my mind, but it definitely took my mind off football."

Coach Butts liked to tell humorous stories about his players. Georgia had four straight losing seasons before they came up with an SEC championship in 1959. The star fullback of that team was a North Carolina mountain boy by the name of Tater Bug Godfrey, and Coach Butts told of the time Tater Bug came up to him after the 1959 season and declared, "Coach, ain't people good to you when you win," imitating Tater Bug's mountain twang to a T.

Another favorite was his story about Derwent Langley, a fine fullback and linebacker from Augusta. One day in practice Langley had failed to carry out a blocking assignment downfield, and when he returned to the huddle, he knew Coach Butts would be ready to take him apart. So he beat him to the punch with "Ain't a'hm the biggest sonafabitch you ever seen, coach?"

Another one was the time he came out of the stadium in Columbus, Georgia (site of the Georgia-Auburn game for many years), after losing to Auburn and he accidentally bumped into a lady. "I beg you pardon, Ma'am," said Coach Butts. "No offense intended." To which the lady replied, "No offense, that's right. And no damn defense either."

Coach Butts' heyday was 1940 through 1948. He had nine straight winners in that span, including three SEC championship teams and two that ranked No. 1 in the nation (1942 and 1946). In that span Georgia and Notre Dame boasted the finest records in the country.

There's no telling how many man-hours Coach Butts and his staff and his players put in giving Georgia those great teams. I know it was around the clock year-round for Coach Butts. How he lived to be 68 is a miracle to me.

The one quality above all others that Coach Butts looked for in a player was what he termed "rattlesnake." By that he meant the pugnacity and fighting spirit that every winner should have. And of all the Bulldogs who ever wore the Red and Black, none had more "rattlesnake" than James Wallace Butts.

Coach Butts was vitally interested in the Georgia football teams under Coach Dooley, who received a letter from Coach Butts every Monday following every game Coach Dooley's teams ever played. When the Bulldogs won, his letters were full of praise. When they lost, he referred to some tough luck the Bulldogs had encountered and he always offered encouragement.

Coach Butts was an avid disciplinarian and he applied this discipline to himself. In recent years he took a daily early-morning jog around Athens, and the last time I saw him was early one morning jogging up Stanton Way, and if I'm not mistaken, he was wearing his pajamas.

Now one of the state of Georgia's greatest sons—certainly its most illustrious native-born-and-bred coach—is buried in Oconee Hills Cemetery overlooking the same Oconee river that flows on down to his boyhood home of Milledgeville.

Even more appropriately, his final resting place is next to Sanford Stadium, which he loved so much.

RIP BUTTS, WONDER DOG

In May, 1976, while I was in Auburn for the SEC tennis tournament, a rain delay gave me time to pay my respects to the Tigers' distinguished athletic director and head football coach, Ralph (Shug) Jordan. Just the previous week he had been honored in ceremonies naming Auburn's football stadium for him.

We chatted about old times in Athens, Shug having spent five years as an assistant football coach under Wallace Butts (1946-50), and he can spin many a yarn about those memorable years highlighted by two SEC championship teams (1946 and 1948). Incidentally, it was in my office that Shug took a phone call from the Auburn president offering him the Tigers' head football job (he didn't want to take this call in his office—a big room shared by all the assistant coaches).

"We had some mighty good football teams at Georgia in those days," recalled Shug. "One of the best was in 1950, and it is not remembered as one of the best because it went 6-2-3, but it easily

Brain trust: (l-r) Shug Jordan, Bill Hartman, Sterling Dupree, Coach Butts, and Rip Butts

could have been undefeated. We had a helluva defense, allowed only 5.5 points per game, but we lost our quarterback (Billy Grant) to an injury in the first game in beating Maryland, 27-7, and Maryland was probably the best team we played. After losing Grant, we never could generate a consistent offense and we averaged only 14.3 points per game."

Coach Jordan rattled off 11 members of that 1950 squad who later played in the NFL: end Harry Babcock, end Johnny Carson, end Bobby Walston, tackle Hamp Tanner, tackle Marion Campbell, tackle Dick Yelvington, guard Nick Feher, defensive back Art De Carlo, defensive back Claude Hipps and running back Billy Mixon. A young soph QB by the name of Zeke Bratkowski was held out that season, but if Coach Butts had played him we might have won the championship.

As I left Coach Jordan's office, he called me back, saying, "I have a rare photograph that you ought to have. It's the only photo I have ever seen of Rip Butts."

Coach Jordan then produced a glossy 8x10 print of Rip Butts (Coach Butts' pet dog, some kind of a terrier, I think), posing with his master, and others in the photo were assistant coaches Jordan, Bill Hartman and Sterling DuPree.

I well recall that Rip Butts used to accompany Coach Butts to his office atop Memorial Hall, and Rip would take part in all the coaches' meetings. Coach Butts would ask all the coaches what they thought of a certain defense, but he would never make a final decision until he had consulted Rip.

Another thing about Rip: he liked to take naps in the backseat of Coach Butts' car, and if Mrs. Butts or any of her daughters (Jean or Faye or Nancy) wanted to borrow the car, they would have to wait until Rip had finished his nap.

"BUMP" GABRIELSEN, THE SHREWD NORWEGIAN

The little Scandinavian country of Norway gave the world the intrepid Vikings and one of football's greatest coaches, Knute Rockne of Notre Dame. It also gave the University of Georgia one of its greatest coaches, Bramwell W. (Bump) Gabrielsen.

"Bump" Gabrielsen

A native of Minnesota, where he had been a star athlete at
Gustavus Adolphus College, Gabrielsen joined the Physical
Education Department staff at Georgia right after World War II.
He was given the additional duty of varsity swimming coach.
Although he didn't have any scholarships, it didn't take him
long to develop teams good enough to dethrone the perennial
Southeastern Conference champions, the Florida Gators, in the
early 1950s.

Having spent many years as a swimmer myself (Athens High and Georgia teams), I was very much interested in the fine job Bump was doing at my alma mater. We formed a close friendship.

Bump was a born coach. He really didn't care anything about scholarships. I know he would not have enjoyed having to beg high school swimmers to accept a scholarship. But he did derive great pleasure in seeing his proteges develop into champions. And I venture to say that no coach has ever done a better job than Bump did with his most famous pupil, Reid Patterson.

Incidentally, Bump, who was a good golfer also, was a very good golf coach and gave private lessons. His daughters Sherry and Bobby Jo and son Jimmy were his most famous golfing proteges, all champions. In fact, Jimmy was runner up in the British Amateur, played on several U.S. Walker Cup teams and became the captain of the U.S. Walker Cup team, and in 1993 was elected to the State of Georgia Sports Hall of Fame.

Bump had a very good sense of humor and I recall him pulling off one of the best jokes I've ever seen. It involved Bump and his identical twin brother, Milton Gabrielsen of New York University, and Col. F. B. Smith, then head of Georgia's Physical Education Department, and Col. Smith's identical twin, Earl Smith of Corning, N.Y.

This episode took place in the early 1950s when both the athletic department and the physical ed department had adjacent offices atop Memorial Hall on the Georgia campus. On this particular day the twin brothers of Coach Gabrielsen and Col. Smith came into my sports information office. Naturally, I thought they were Coach Gabrielsen and Col. Smith, and I greeted them as usual. Finally, I noticed the smirks on their faces, and Coach Gabrielsen and Col. Smith walked into the office grinning like Cheshire cats. It was quite a shock to me.

I thought this act had wonderful possibilities. So I persuaded the two sets of twins to pull their stunt on Coach Wallace Butts: the out-of-town twins confronted the unsuspecting Butts and complained about the niggardly budget Coach Butts allowed the swimming team. Needless to say, Coach Butts was about to throw them out of his office until the other twins came in.

Coach Gabrielsen and Col. Smith pulled an even bolder stunt on their golfing confrere, University President O.C. Aderhold.

The out-of-town twins went into Dr. Adherhold's office and after a rather brief chat demanded that their salaries be raised immediately. Needless to say, Dr. Aderhold was more than a little ruffled, but just before he had the twins ushered out of his office, the real Coach Gabrielsen and Col. Smith came in and saved the day. Dr. Aderhold had quite a good laugh, too.

There is one more part to that story. Had Dr. Aderhold agreed to their demands for a salary raise, Coach Gabrielsen and Col. Smith would not have joined their twins in Dr. Aderhold's office.

STERLING DUPREE, THE NOBLEST OF THEM ALL

If ever a man were aptly named it was Sterling DuPree, who throughout his distinguished career personified the dictionary's definition of the adjective *sterling*: "of the highest quality."

This native southwest Georgian from the flatlands of Worth county was installed in the State of Georgia Athletic Hall of Fame because of brilliant performances as a sprinter in track and fullback in football and a highly successful career as a collegiate coach in the same sports. But he could have qualified for any kind of Hall of Fame because of his unimpeachable character. Truly, he was deserving of Shakespeare's immortal epithet in his *Julius Caesar*, "the noblest Roman of them all."

Looking back on 45 years' association with Sterling DuPree, I recall my first glimpse (and that's about all one could get of him when he was in full stride) of the South's fastest sprinter and the world's fastest white man, as he was later tagged, winning the 100- and 220-yard dashes for Auburn in a dual match against Georgia on the old cinder track that now is a parking lot by the main entrance to Sanford Stadium; watching him run the football and back up the line (they played both ways in his day) against Georgia in Columbus as his Tigers completed an undefeated season in 1932 and claimed the Southern championship; covering the Southern AAU track meet in Atlanta for the *Atlanta Journal* and chatting with him about his protege, Scooter Rucks of South Carolina, who went on to win the NCAA 440-yard dash;

Coach Dupree with (l-r) Tommy Lawrence, Bill Stanfill, and Tim Callaway

marveling at the great backfield he coached at Florida in 1949, led by All-American Charley Hunsinger, a crew that humbled Georgia in Jacksonville, 28-7.

Watching him work with Zeke Bratkowski, teaching this slow-footed but strong-armed passer to fade back quickly into the pocket from which he would later set SEC passing records en route to an outstanding professional career highlighted by world's championships with the Green Bay Packers; picking muscadines with him and his family (Alda and Barbara) at Moody's vineyards near Maxeys, Georgia; introducing Barbara to the game of tennis and watching her develop into the state's No. 1 women's player, also a beauty queen at Georgia and a Phi Beta Kappa scholar.

Watching him, after he had laid down his coaching mantle, recruit so many outstanding young players that he was a vital cog in Georgia's magnificent football success under Vince Dooley.

The Georgia Bulldogs will be indebted forever to Sterling DuPree for his numerous contributions to the cause, but personally I consider his No. 1 contribution as having been made in the fall of 1957. The Red and Black flag was not flying high in those days; indeed, it was at half-mast. The Enemy had conquered Georgia's proud football forces eight straight years. Our great chieftain, Wallace Butts, assigned to Coach DuPree the task of "breaking the enemy's code," so to speak. It was a tough assignment. The Golden Tornado, from 1951 through 1956, had run roughshod over almost everybody in becoming one of the nation's football powerhouses. But Coach DuPree scouted them every game that season of 1957, and on November 30, on Grant Field in Atlanta, a superbly prepared and resolute band of Bulldogs shut out the Jackets, 7-0, and broke the drought. The opportunity to win came early in the third quarter when Tech fumbled and Theron Sapp recovered at midfield. Sapp carried nine times in the game-winning drive and was the real hero, but the key play was a pass play on third and 11. Sterling DuPree sent in the play, special instructions to Charley Britt not to throw a long pass but just enough for the first down, and to "get that ball to Jimmy Orr," who was about the surest receiver in the game. Britt did "get that ball to Orr," who snagged it going out of bounds and made the first down by inches, but it might as well have been a mile as far as The Enemy was concerned.

Coach DuPree, in addition to having enjoyed a very successful career as a backfield coach, scout and recruiter, was certainly one of the most popular fellows in the coaching profession. He possessed a keen sense of humor and was a great story teller.

The late Perron Shoemaker (assistant coach with DuPree at Georgia) used to enjoy telling this story about DuPree which took place when both were on Bear Wolf's staff at Florida in the years right after World War II:

DuPree and Shoemaker were traveling through the state of Florida on a recruiting trip when they had to stop at a service station to get their car's fan belt repaired. While the service station attendant was working on their car, Coach DuPree noticed that the man's wife spoke with a German accent, and he asked her if she were from Germany. She replied, "Yah," and DuPree then began telling her of his war experiences in Germany with Gen. Patton's famed Third Army.

DuPree would ask her if she knew of such and such a town in Germany, and she would reply, "Yah, yah." And then DuPree would declare each time, "Well, I took that town."

This went on for about 10 minutes, following which the lady ran to her husband and hollered, "Fritz! Fritz! Come quick and see the man vat wan the war!"

VINCE DOOLEY

Coach Vince Dooley has a good sense of humor and appreciates a good joke, but he is strictly business during his football drills. This great chieftain is smart and tough, and he had the boyhood background to be tough. He grew up on the streets of Mobile and spent several years of his youth with a gang of toughs. But he was "saved" from this gang life by athletics and by a high school coach who gave him an alternate outlook on life.

Dooley was a strong boy and he could whip any other boy or rival in town, usually by throwing them in a wrestling maneuver rather than by fisticuffs, he once told me. His toughest rival soon became his younger brother Bill, who was very strong and destined to be bigger than he. And it was Bill's ambition to whip his brother Vince, who had left Mobile and gone to Auburn on a football scholarship to play QB. A couple of years later Bill won a football scholarship to Mississippi State and he put on 20 pounds. When he returned home that summer he challenged older brother Vince to a wrestling match. Vince looked at his brother, who was no longer "Baby Bill" but by now a bigger and stronger

Bill Dooley with "little brother" Vince Dooley

physical specimen than he, a typical big lineman, much more menacing than a quarterback. Vince said to Bill: "I think we have outgrown this kid stuff. I have more serious things to do."

That is a good example of how astute Vince Dooley was even as a college boy.

———— ■ ————

(The following remarks were made by Magill at a roast honoring Coach Dooley given by the Juvenile Diabetes Foundation International.)

Many coaches are superstitious, including Coach Dooley, who always changes hotels if his team loses. Come to think of it, that may be another reason he retired from coaching; there wasn't a single hotel within a 50-mile radius of Auburn, Alabama, where he would book his Bulldogs.

A few years ago, Georgia hadn't beaten Clemson at Death Valley in a number of years. So Coach Dooley ordered the Bulldogs to wear special red britches against Clemson in order to break the spell. It worked. We won.

After the game, the sportswriters asked Coach Dooley, "Do you think the red britches really had anything to do with Georgia's victory?" And Coach Dooley, although I am positive that he really thought the red britches were a vital factor, replied with a straight face: "Absolutely not. It's not the color of the pants that wins ball games; it's what the players do in those pants."

Coach Dooley used to like to play tennis. In the summer of '64 he came out to our courts and asked me if anybody was around who could give him a good workout. So I introduced him to an old Athens player, Mr. Howard Shelton, following which Coach Dooley took me aside and said, "Haven't you got someone younger?" I replied, "I'm sorry, he's the only player available, but he'll give you a good workout." Mr. Shelton, who was state 70-year old champion, won every game.

I could detect that Coach Dooley was mad about being humiliated by this old man, and he stayed away from the courts several weeks. Finally, he showed up one day and he said he didn't want to play any old man. It so happened that the only player available was a little Athens boy who was quite small even for his age of 12. Again Coach Dooley called me aside said, "For God's sake, is this little boy the only player here?" I replied: "Yes, but he'll give you a good workout." The little boy won, 6-0, 6-0. His name was Danny Birchmore, then the Georgia state champion 12-and-under, who went on to win the U.S. Boys' 18 clay courts title, beating Jimmy Connors on the way, and also made All-America twice at Georgia. He is now a doctor—a rheumatologist—in Delaware.

Danny Birchmore

Coach Dooley has not played on our courts again. "Football knee," he says!

I must say I am surprised to see so many Georgia Tech people participating in such a worthwhile undertaking as the prevention of juvenile diabetes, and I want to say to them right off the bat that I deeply resent the slurring remarks they made about Coach Dooley when he was contemplating running for Emperor—I mean governor. I refer to the new stanza they added to their famous fight song:

> I'm a rambling wreck from Georgia Tech
> And a helluva engineer;
> If Dooley thinks I'll vote for him,
> He can stick it in his ear.

You know, Coach Dooley and I both retired from active coaching last year. I did it first, and then he copied me. I thought about running for president of the United States, but when the FBI sent a hooker down to entrap me, she succeeded.

There's been much speculation about why Vince decided not to run for governor. Besides the fact that he's not a native Georgian, that he never went to school in Georgia, that he never held a public office, that he has never been elected to office, that he'd be a Catholic campaigning in the Bible Belt of the South, that not a single Tech man would vote for him, and that after he quit Georgia damned few Bulldogs were gonna vote for him . . . besides all that, the main reason he withdrew was that he was running on the wrong ticket. He was running as a Democrat, but he realized that he embraces the ideology of the Republicans.

Twenty-five years ago "Vince Who?" was the big question being bandied about. Barbara Dooley in her inimitable way tells the priceless story of trying to locate Vince at a meeting shortly after he arrived in Athens. Since he was a newcomer and unknown, she was asked to describe him.

"Well, he's a little bit short, a little bit fat, a little bit bald, and he has a big nose." And with that graphic description Vince was immediately located.

Now a quarter of a century later, Vincent Joseph Dooley is not a "little bit short." He is a giant of a man, towering over his peers; seven times SEC coach of the year, six times district coach-of-the-year, twice national couch of the year, and president of the

National Football Coaches' Association—Vince Dooley stands tall.

He is not "a little bit fat," but is "lean as a bean" and, despite a little trouble with his ticker, he appears in better shape than ever. He also has cut the fat from the Athletic Department. During his tenure the UGA Athletic Association has donated millions to non-athletic activities at the university.

Not only has Coach Dooley accomplished such feats as whipping Notre Dame for the national championship, but he has also achieved the even more remarkable feat (especially from my vantage point) of appearing to have more hair on his head today than he did 25 years ago. Does he walk on water? It would surely seem so.

Unlike Pinocchio, whose nose grew longer as he was bad and told untruths, Vince's nose has seemed to grow shorter—or at least more Grecian—as his strengths and accomplishments and good deeds have become evident to all.

For years he has worked tirelessly for crippled children in Georgia through the Easter Seals program. By tightening scholastic requirements for student athletes, he has emphasized the value of a college education; by introducing drug-testing for student athletes, he has helped deter the spread of drug use on campus.

What this really boils down to and what I'm trying to say is that after 25 years we really love this man—warts and all.

———— ■ ————

(And the following comes from Magill's remarks at a roast honoring Coach Dooley given by the Georgia Heart Association.)

I think this "Big Heart" Award for Coach Dooley is most inappropriate. It ought to be the "Big Nose" Award.

Coach Devine of Notre Dame was so eager to play Georgia in the Sugar Bowl he said he would push a peanut with his nose all the way to New Orleans for the chance to play us. As soon as I read that in the paper, I called the Associated Press and said that Georgia was so anxious to play Notre Dame that Coach Dooley would push a watermelon with his nose all the way to New Orleans — without bending over.

Seriously, Coach Dooley's great record at Georgia has inspired me to write, with the help of my daughter Sharon, the following poem entitled: "Vince Who?"

When Dooley was announced in sixty-four
To lead the Bulldogs to the top once more,
Vince Who? was all the alumni asked.
Who in the world is that jack-ass?

A War Eagle? Why, he's a traitor at best,
He'll never stand up to the test.
How could a pipe-smoking, scholarly fellow
Ever prepare us for the white and yellow?

But 17 years later we hold our heads high
And thank our lucky stars we got this guy.

Georgia's now no. 1, at the top of the chart,
And thanks to Zachry's Men's Store
Vince is dressed to play the part.

Coach of the Year said AP and UP
The MacArthur Cup, the Stegeman Cup, king
   of the SEC

Glory, glory to ol' Georgia,
Proudly plays the Red Coat Band;

Glory, glory to St. Vincent
Who's led us to the Promised Land.

Now besieged by requests and reporters galore,
The Athletic Department tries to please all once more

An announcement is made–Vince will see you at two.
A moment of dead silence, then comes a voice from
   the blue.

"Vince? Vince Who?
It's Herschel Walker we came to interview."

Loran Smith (l) with Upshaw Bentley, Dan Magill, Vince Dooley, and Larry Young
(Magill holds official proclamation naming Magill Creek in 1977)

Chapter Five

A MAGILL MISCELLANY

LORAN SMITH ROAST

Loran Smith, author of two of the best books on Georgia football, *Glory! Glory!* and *Between the Hedges,* came to Georgia in the fall of 1955 on a freshman Ag scholarship awarded by Sears Roebuck Co. He had no idea of pursuing a writing career. He had grown up on his father's farm (cotton, corn, peanuts). But he always did love sports and he had done a lot of reading in his county library. He had especially enjoyed sports books on the lives of Babe Ruth and Lou Gehrig.

Looking back, Loran recalls that he enjoyed writing letters to people, but he didn't realize then that this was an early indication that he had writing in his blood. He actually wrote his first story when he was a senior in high school. He was elected the reporter for his senior class when they took the annual seniors' trip to the nation's capital, and he wrote a three-part series about it that was featured in the *Wrightsville Headlight,* his county's weekly newspaper.

Although he certainly had a farm boy's background, Loran didn't like Ag School at Georgia. He remembers that a girl he had dated back home once had suggested to him that he major in journalism at Georgia because he had written such a fine article on the seniors' trip to Washington. When he finally told his Ag School advisor, Dr. Robert Wheeler, that he had always enjoyed writing, Dr. Wheeler advised him to transfer to the Journalism School.

While in Journalism school, he hung around the *Red and Black,* the school newspaper. He became sports editor and circulation manager. He also worked in my office at sports information, and he went out for the track team and was good enough for Coach Towns to give him a part scholarship. Coach Towns also got him a job serving in the "chow line" at Payne Hall, then the athletes' dorm. He was given a free room at Reed Hall for sorting the mail. He really worked his way through college.

Loran has received high praise for his books, and I believe the highest accolade for him would be to say that he is as gifted at writing as his fellow townsman from Wrightsville, Herschel Walker, is at toting the football. It is an amazing coincidence that a product of a small country town could be the main cog in Georgia's national championship team and that his deeds would be glorified by a fellow Johnson Countian.

I well remember when Loran came down to my old sports information office in Stegeman Hall back in the 1950s and asked me for a job. He said he would work for "free" and that he just wanted experience and to learn to be a sportswriter. He was dressed in the scanty uniform given members of the Georgia freshman track team, on which he ran the mile and later set the school record. He wore that track uniform to my office every day that fall, and I really believe that uniform constituted his entire wardrobe. I was so concerned about him that I brought him some of my old clothes, which at first he refused, being a proud fellow. But then I told him that he should accept them because that would be his only payment for helping me, and, besides, I reminded him, that winter soon would be coming.

We used to have a lot of fun up at Harry's, the old tavern at Five Points. Loran was so emaciated—either from not eating or running too much on the track or both—that I began taking him to Harry's along with the out of town sportswriters, and we'd have supper there. I learned there that he was a gifted storyteller and a great joke-teller, especially after a few beers and some good food. He really entertained the visiting writers with his jokes and pretty soon he began upstaging me at every opportunity. He would get quite uppity after a few beers.

I remember how deathly afraid he was of his track coach, Speck Towns. He referred to him (behind his back, of course) as The Bear. Later Speck used to refer to Loran as my "gofer" and still later Speck teased him by saying he had risen from being "gofer" for me to the status of being "bird dog" for both Coach Dooley and Coach Hartman.

I recall when Johnny Griffith succeeded Coach Butts as head football coach, and then Johnny named our mutual friend, Jim Whatley, his administrative assistant. At that time Loran was sports editor of the *Red and Black*. He wrote a letter to Coach Griffith offering his services to the athletic department. He said he could help in recruiting, publicity, anything, and that he just wanted to help his alma mater. Coach Whatley answered the letter for Coach Griffith and wrote: "Dear Mr. Smith, Thank you for your letter and offer to help. I have decided that the best way you can help Georgia's athletic department is to stay as far away from it as possible. Thank you for nothing. Sincerely, Johnny Griffith."

Loran is now a famous man, probably the only American who is listed in Webster's dictionary not once but thrice as a synonym for *unpunctual, unavailable* and *chronic name-dropper*.

By the way, I have just finished my latest book, entitled *Great Name-Droppers I Have Known,* and my first chapter is devoted to him. I told about the time I was in Loran's office during the week of the Masters and he was moaning, "Damn it, I need some more Masters tickets and Jack can't help me anymore." I said, "Jack Who?" and he replied, "Nicklaus." Then he added, "I've got a call into Arnie. He owes me a favor." But his cake-taker, I think, was the time he came back from a Bulldog Club meeting in Washington, DC, which was at the time President Reagan was shot, and he told me, "Dan, I was at The House when we got word about The Chief."

JOEL EAVES

The flags at the Butts-Mehre building (the Georgia Bulldogs' athletic headquarters) flew at half-mast in tribute to Joel Harry Eaves when he passed away. Without a doubt, his 16-year leadership of Georgia's athletic program (November 1963-July 1979) was one of the most outstanding AD jobs ever done anywhere.

He made numerous contributions while at the Bulldogs' helm, but the most important achievement was the rescue of our sinking football ship, whose three straight losing seasons in 1961-63 had caused serious financial problems and a low morale among all Bulldogs. His surprise choice of a comparatively unknown and young freshman coach, Vince Dooley, to lead Georgia out of the wilderness raised eyebrows at first, but not for long. Dooley, in his first season in 1964, broke a three-year drought against Georgia Tech, took the Bulldogs to their first bowl game in five years and was named SEC Coach-of-the-Year. He went on to compile the finest record of any Georgia football coach in history and one of the best ever in the nation.

Coach Eaves did more for Georgia football than hitting the jackpot with Vince Dooley. He improved the looks of Sanford Stadium, always a naturally beautiful place. He immediately

Joel Eaves flanked by Coach Dooley and Gov. Carl Sanders

removed the ugly light poles and discontinued night games. He was the first Georgia athletic director to believe that the football budget could be balanced by playing more than three or four home games a year in Sanford Stadium. In fact, he arranged the schedule to include six or seven games a year in Sanford Stadium. He also didn't like the inequitable contract Georgia had with Florida for its annual game in Jacksonville. He threatened to take the game out of Jacksonville unless Georgia got a 50-50 break on number of tickets and location. He won. He also improved the Georgia Tech contract, getting Georgia a 50-50 deal in that game for the first time ever.

He worked to get Georgia improved facilities. The long-needed coliseum was dedicated February 22, 1964 with a basketball victory over Georgia Tech. McWhorter Hall, home of Bulldog athletes, was built. Sanford Stadium was double-decked. Major improvements were made at the baseball field and the track. He authorized the building of Henry Feild tennis stadium in 1977, launching the campaign that resulted in Georgia eventually having the finest collegiate tennis setup in the country.

He improved the budgets for all sports and made it possible for all Georgia teams to compete for the SEC championship. He demanded that Georgia representatives in athletics be well-groomed and proud to wear the Red and Black.

He insisted that Georgia athletes do well in the classroom and there was an immediate upsurge in grades. Many Georgia athletes have been honored nationally and regionally for their academic excellence.

Georgia athletic teams, during his 16 years as AD, compiled a brilliant won-lost percentage of .722 and won 19 SEC team championships. He also balanced the budget, a matter of no small importance and a feat his predecessors seldom had been able to accomplish.

When he retired, he relinquished the leadership reins to his most famous protege, Vince Dooley, fully confident that he would do as fine a job as AD as he did as football coach. He was right again.

Joel Eaves was not only a great man in the athletic world. He was a great American, one of the last of a special but vanishing breed who have done tremendous good for this country by molding strong characters of American boys in athletics.

He knew athletics inside-out. I was privileged to know him throughout his long career in athletics, first seeing him in the early 1930s when he represented Tech High of Atlanta in the state high school basketball tournament in old Woodruff Hall. A few years later I saw him wearing the blue and orange of the Auburn Plainsmen against the Red and Black of Georgia in football at Columbus, in basketball at Woodruff Hall, and baseball at old Sanford Field. He was a superb athlete.

I had the opportunity to know him well right after World War II when he returned to Atlanta, beginning his coaching career in high school there when I was prep sports editor of the *Atlanta Journal.* His fine records at Murphy High caught the attention of Auburn's athletic director Wilbur Hutsell, who lured him back to his alma mater as an assistant football coach and head basketball coach. He was so outstanding at Auburn that his reputation caused the Georgia athletic board to bring him to Athens.

Tall and erect as an Indian chief, with a handsome grey head of hair, Joel Eaves looked the part of a great chieftain. He was tall in the saddle and a straight shooter—respected and loved by all who knew him.

Barbara Dooley Sauté

When the Dooleys first arrived on the Georgia scene 27 years ago, the question everyone asked was "VINCE WHO?" But that was soon followed by "BARBARA WOO HOO!"

When I first met Barbara she was expecting her first child. I remember thinking she didn't look old enough. Today she is the grandmother of five grandchildren. She still doesn't look old enough.

I remember when my daughter Mollie and her best friend, Mary Beth McDonald, used to play Broadway show tunes on their record-player all day long, no doubt dreaming of being on Broadway some day. One of those songs, from *Sound of Music,* reminds me of Barbara:

Barbara Dooley

How do you solve a problem like Maria?
How do you catch a cloud and pin it down?
How do you find a word that means Maria?
A flippity jibet, a will of the wisp, a clown.

Barbara is like Maria. She's quicksilver, a will of the wisp. She's hard to pin down. For example, she's pious—on her knees pious. And yet . . . she's highly irreverent, making some of the most outlandish remarks ever heard.

She's a devout Catholic—on her knees Catholic. And yet . . . she says she's a born again Christian.

Her daily life is based on athletics. The very bread on her table is derived from sports—and yet . . . Barbara herself is something of a klutz at athletics.

She is very knowledgeable about nutrition and proper eating habits. And yet . . . Barbara is so thin that people are forever asking, "Is she anorexic?"

We know her as Barbara . . . but . . . growing up in Birmingham she was called Barbara Ann. We know her husband as Vince . . . but . . . to Barbara he's always called Vincent. Barbara wisely proclaims Vincent as the head of the Dooley household . . . but, everyone in Athens knows that Barbara is the Queen Bee—except possibly Ol' Vince himself.

In spite of the many contradictions about Barbara that leave us all in a spin, she has some traits that never vary, the foremost being that Barbara has never met a stranger. She is a people person who can talk to anyone and outtalk anyone. She delights in making friends with everyone.

During their first year at Georgia when Vince was earning that highly publicized salary of $18,000 per year, the workmen on the Dooley home were so smitten with Barbara (and felt like such close friends of the family) that they bought winter jackets for her children.

A few years later when the Junior League was soliciting Christmas toys for needy children, Barbara sweet-talked Sears into almost underwriting the entire project. And as is typical of Barbara, in appreciation she then bought all of her children's toys, including four bicycles, from her new-found friends at Sears.

Vince's good relations with the press are attributable in no small way to Barbara, who is any journalist's dream: outgoing and always good copy.

Besides her friendly loquacious manner, Barbara's sense of humor and wit are outstanding. In fact, so keen is her sense of humor that Barbara is the only female I know—the *only* female I know—whom I could poke fun at—even gently—in public and not pay for it the rest of my life.

When Barbara found herself unexpectedly pregnant for a

fifth time, someone asked, "What in the world happened?" To which Barbara replied, "Well, Vincent thought I was on the pill, and I thought he was over the hill."

One of the best received stories Barbara now tells at touchdown club meetings throughout the South is about the cheerleaders at little Shelbyville, Tennessee, high school. They won the national cheerleaders' contest with their never-to-be-forgotten chant:

"Shelbyville! Shelbyville! We are it!
SH for Shelbyville! IT for it!"

We tend to think of success in terms of being an eminent doctor, a corporate lawyer, the CEO of a large company, or *possibly* the winningest coach in tennis. But I like Emerson's definition of success and I think Emerson must have had Barbara in mind when he wrote this:

> To laugh often and love much; to win the respect of intelligent people and the affection of children; to earn the approbation of honest citizens; to appreciate beauty; to find the best in others; to give of one's self; to leave the world a bit better, whether by a healthy child, a garden patch or a redeemed social condition; to have played and laughed with enthusiasm and sung with exultation; to know even one life has breathed easier because you have lived—this is to have succeeded.

I think Barbara has been highly successful. Don't you?

CHARLIE MARTIN'S HEDGES

"Between the hedges" is a proud slogan, indeed, for the Georgia Bulldog people, although no one seems to know who originated it. But one thing is for sure: there would be no such saying if the late Charlie Martin had not had the bright idea of planting the hedge of privet ligustrum around the field shortly after Sanford Stadium was built in 1929.

There never lived a more loyal Georgia Bulldog than Charles E. Martin, who came to Athens in the fall of 1908, fresh out of

Culloden High School in Monroe county, and the first thing he saw on the campus was a game he had never seen before in his life. Immediately, he fell in love with it and later he became one of its biggest promoters.

"When I stepped off the train on my first trip to Athens," Charlie told me back in the 1950s when I wrote an article about him, "I met a Mr. Fitzpatrick, who was supposed to escort me to his boarding house off Lumpkin street, but he took me on a detour, insisting that I watch a game of football being played on the campus in front of the chapel bell on a field named for the chemistry professor, Dr. Charles Herty, who had introduced football to Georgia in 1892.

"Baseball was the major sport in those days," Charlie continued, "and it was especially popular at Georgia because of its Southern championship team in the spring of 1908. Baseball receipts actually helped finance the football program in those days (as football certainly does now for almost all the other sports, men and women). I was so fascinated by football that very first day that I really thought it might eventually prove to be more popular than even baseball."

While in college Charlie became a "sporting writer" for the old *Athens Banner* and was a campus sports correspondent for the old *Atlanta Georgian*. It was his good fortune to have been in Athens during the legendary football career of Georgia's first All-American, Bob McWhorter. Charlie wrote so much about McWhorter that he was known as "McWhorter's Boswell."

After graduation at Georgia, Charlie returned to his home in middle Georgia, but he loved Athens so much he came back to study law. He got sidetracked, however, and ended up back at the *Athens Banner.* His journalism career was interrupted by World War I, during which he served overseas in France with the 53rd Infantry Division, attaining the rank of captain. He commanded a company in the Vosges and Argonne sectors.

Although he never played on an athletic team at Georgia, Charlie later became a golf addict and was one of the leading players in town. His first love remained Georgia football, though, and he eventually began work in the Georgia athletic department as business manager in 1927. He became a staunch friend of athletic director Herman Stegeman, football coach

George (Kid) Woodruff and President S. V. Sanford, a most avid supporter of intercollegiate athletics.

In those days, Georgia had to play its archrival Georgia Tech on Grant Field in Atlanta because old Sanford Field, which was built for baseball, seated only 10,000, while Grant Field seated some 28,000. And football had grown to such a high degree of popularity that old Sanford Field simply could not seat all the fans who wanted to see the Georgia-Georgia Tech game.

Finally, Dr. Sanford's dream of having "the best football stadium in Dixie" on the University of Georgia campus was realized. And what an opponent was scheduled for the dedicatory game! Mighty Yale, longtime scourge of the East, came to the South for the first time in its history, and it was Charlie Martin who was the main promoter of this great event. Over 30,000 fans (largest crowd in the history of Southern football at the time) came to Athens for that historic game.

In 1960, Charlie published a book of his Georgia football memoirs, entitled *I've Seen 'Em All*, and, indeed he had seen all the greats of Dixie football for half a century.

In 1970 Charlie passed away at age 82. How I wish he could have been with us in 1992 to celebrate the Georgia football centennial. He made many contributions to his alma mater and will always be remembered for having the privet ligustrum hedge planted back in 1929. It is a beautiful legacy from a wonderful Georgia Bulldog.

MORGAN BLAKE, SPORTS EDITOR

I began writing sports at a very early age, and I thought I was a boy wonder. But the wonder of it was that my dad (the editor of the *Athens Banner-Herald*) allowed my stuff to get in print. I must admit, though, that he never paid me. In fact, I wrote for the *Banner-Herald* some 10 years and was never paid a penny. I was given two picture show passes a week at a time when tickets cost a quarter apiece.

During the Depression years of the 1930s, times were tough, but I didn't know it then. I had no idea that things could be better.

In those days one of the most renowned sportswriters in the South was the veteran sports editor of the *Atlanta Journal*, Morgan Blake, who wrote a column entitled "Sportanic Eruptions." Mr. Blake actually was a little man, much smaller than I had imagined. I finally had the opportunity to meet him when I traveled to Atlanta by bus to ask him in person for a job as campus correspondent for the *Journal.*

My dad knew Mr. Blake. They had worked together a year on the *Journal* right after World War I, and my dad arranged the appointment for me. I am not a self-made man.

I had no idea that Mr. Blake was a champion practical joker, and when I arrived in the *Journal* sports department everyone on the floor (except me) knew that I was "fresh meat" for Mr. Blake—in fact, his first offering of the day.

I was welcomed into the sports office by a former Georgia baseball player, John Martin, who was in the "slot." John later became famous as an outdoor writer and wrote a column with the unforgettable title, "Inside Outdoors."

John first introduced me to other well-known sportswriters like O. B. Keeler (Bobby Jones' "Boswell"), Guy Butler (expert on the Atlanta Crackers) and Ed Miles (Georgia Tech expert who later succeeded Mr. Keeler as the golf writer). Then John told me that Mr. Blake unfortunately had been in bad health the past few days and was suffering from nausea, and had a very bad upset stomach right that moment.

I said, "I'm so sorry. Perhaps I should come back another time."

Then I heard a man coughing in the next room. John Martin leaned over and whispered to me, "That's Mr. Blake. He's having another seizure."

Just at that moment Mr. Blake came out of his office coughing, and staggered right over to where I was sitting. Suddenly he stopped, leaned over me and from his mouth unfurled a yellow tape-measure. Of course, I didn't know it was a yellow tape measure at that time. I thought it was something else and jumped a mile high to get out of the way. And, as I jumped, everyone on the floor laughed like a hyena and my face turned red as a beet.

Then Mr. Blake stuck out his hand and said, "No hard feelings, young man."

I shook his hand, which had an electric thing concealed in it, and it shocked the heck out of me. Again just everybody on the floor about died laughing.

Finally, Mr. Blake put his arm around my shoulder and took me into his office and said, "Sit down, my boy, and tell me the news from Athens."

So I sat down in this big cushioned chair, and when I sat on the cushion a loud noise erupted like air coming out of an automobile tire innertube.

Again everyone on the floor roared with laughter—all except me. I really don't remember much that happened afterwards because I was pretty close to being in a state of shock. But Mr. Blake did let me have the job. I guess I had earned it.

THE INCOMPARABLE "STEGE"

I will always remember H. J. (Herman Jerome) Stegeman, who was Georgia's athletic director when I was a boy and dean of men when I was a freshman at Georgia in 1938. He was a husky, blond Dutchman, out of Holland, Michigan, who wore wooden shoes as a boy. He was Amos Alonzo Stagg's greatest all-round athlete at the University of Chicago when Chicago was the most powerful athletic establishment in the country.

Stege was a great prankster, too. Perhaps the best one he ever pulled off was back in October, 1929, when Yale came down to Athens to dedicate Sanford Stadium. Stege took the New York sportswriters to the Athens Country Club for a round of golf the day before the game, and after one of the holes Stege changed the marker for the next hole so that the tee shot required a water carry of over 300 yards. When the New York scribes looked out over the lake, one of them groaned, "My God! That's the longest water carry I've ever seen!"

Stege replied, "Oh, it's not nearly as long as it looks."

The Eastern writers lost over a dozen balls in the lake before they noticed Stege doubling over with laughter.

——— ■ ———

Herman Stegeman

Stege also used to win bets from the New York sportswriters when Georgia played Fordham and NYU in Yankee Stadium during the early 1930s. He would say to them, "We have with us a boy who can throw the football over 100 yards," and the Eastern writers immediately offered to bet big money that it couldn't be done. Then Stege would call over Georgia's water boy, who was the star fastball pitcher of the Athens Negro baseball team— Clegg Stark —and Clegg would stand on the goal line and hurl the ball sidearmed a little over the length of the field, while Stege would go around collecting his bets. It was known as the "Stege and Clegg" act.

THE BIG SNAKE FIGHT

Although it has been almost 60 years since "The Big Snake Fight" was held at the old UGA tennis courts on a hot summer's day in the late 1930s, I still get occasional queries from people who have heard about it.

In the Depression days of the 1930s, well before television, there was not a whole lot of entertainment available for the common folk, and promoters came up with many strange divisions (like marathon dance contests). And I had the brainstorm to put on a king snake-rattlesnake fight for the "snake championship of the world."

It was a coincidence that I had captured a giant king snake that summer and my good friend, Herschel Carithers, had also captured a huge timber rattler. Both of us had learned all about snakes from the renowned Ross Allen, who as a young man was the waterfront and nature study director at the Athens YMCA Camp for Boys in the Georgia mountains above Tallulah Falls.

It was not unusual for Ross Allen's legion of Athens "disciples" to go snake-hunting in the woods around Athens to see who could catch the most snakes. It was on such an expedition that I had captured my king snake in a creek by the Athens YWCA girls' camp in Oconee County. It measured 74 inches long (six feet, two inches) and it so excited me that I telephoned Ross Allen at his headquarters in Silver Springs, Florida, and asked him if I had caught a record sized king snake. Ross replied that it was, indeed, pretty close to the record length of a king snake but that he was pretty damned busy at the moment checking a cargo of pit vipers he had just received from Central America. Incidentally, Ross himself had captured the largest diamondback rattler on record (over eight feet long) near Thomasville, Georgia, and also the largest cottonmouth water moccasin (over six feet long) near Savannah, Georgia, not to mention the largest American alligator on record (over 14 feet long) in Lake George near Ocala, Florida. Of course, Ross was most famous for being John Weissmueller's double in the Tarzan movies (it was Ross who wrestled the "crocodiles"—really big Florida Gators—not Weissmueller). And Grantland Rice once wrote a story about Ross, calling him the "real Tarzan."

Herschel had captured his big rattler at the Athens Y Camp in Rabun County and it measured a little over five feet, about as big as timber rattlers get, and at the end of camp that summer he pedalled his bicycle back home to Athens (some 60 miles) with the rattlesnake in a croker sack tied to the handlebars of his bicycle. That was quite a feat in itself, but nothing special for Herschel, who was a most gifted young man. As a matter of fact, Herschel later left the university to join the U.S. Army Air Force (in the days when the Air Force was part of the Army). Germany was on the rampage in Europe and a world war was looming, one that Herschel didn't want to miss. He became one of America's crack pilots and served as Averill Harriman's personal pilot when Mr. Harriman was U.S. Ambassador to Moscow during World War II. And, still much later, in 1963, when Georgia's basketball coliseum was just a skeleton (only the big concrete roof had been built), he flew a small airplane smack through the building—a tremendous feat which he never admitted to because it was against the law. But I know he did it because I saw it.

But back to The Big Snake fight:

When Herschel returned home with his prize, he proudly brought it up to Harry's Tavern at Five Points in Athens, which was a special hangout for Athens boys—and older men, too. It so happened that I already had my king snake on display in a cage there, and it didn't take long for us to get into an argument over which snake could whip the other. Finally, I issued an official challenge, saying that my snake would defend his championship against the "big-mouthed" challenger from Rabun County. King snakes generally are considered the champion snake fighters since they can wrap around the other snakes, crush them and them gobble them up.

I had access to space in the *Athens Banner-Herald*, where my father was the editor, and I wrote a story saying that there would be a "big snake fight" at the UGA tennis courts at high noon that coming Saturday, admission 10 cents. We had a pretty good crowd of 200 or so, and I do believe every police officer in town was there from both the city and county forces. I had to admit them free.

I had built a wooden ring on the center tennis court, about 10 feet square and one foot high. I served as the announcer and the referee, and introduced the combatants as they do at heavyweight championship fights: "In this corner, in black, brown and yellow skin, sporting 10 rattles and a button, at five feet, one inch and . . . pounds (I can't remember his weight but he was heavier than the king snake), the scourge of Rabun County, the deadly poisonous Rastus Rattlesnake . . . [a lot of applause] . . . and his opponent, in resplendent ebony black and milk white skin, the pride of Oconee County, at six foot, two inches and . . . pounds, the defending snake champion of the world, Casper King Snake . . . [more applause] . . . you snakes know the rules, at the sound of the whistle, come out fighting."

I then blew the whistle, but they did not come out fighting. Instead they remained motionless in opposite corners of the ring, the rattler in his famous coil, head poised, ready to strike, and they constantly flicked their tongues in order to hear.

Some of the fans yelled that they wanted their money back. As referee and promoter, I felt it my duty to get the snakes to fight. So, with my forked stick (to be used to catch them and return them to their respective cages when and if necessary), I prodded each snake, hollering at them, "Come on, you damned snakes, mix it up . . . FIGHT." And when I prodded the rattler he struck at me with such ferocity that I jumped at least five feet in the air and plum out of the ring, barely escaping his fangs. This caused a great cheer from the spectators and seemed to satisfy those who had asked for their money back.

But the damned snakes would not fight. Undoubtedly, they were frightened by the crowd of people (they are just as fearful of people as most people are afraid of them). The crowd gradually left, all except me and Herschel and Clegg Stark, who had come up the hill from Sanford Stadium. (His son, Clegg Jr., by the way, used to help me at the tennis courts.) Well, Herschel and I decided to put both snakes in Herschel's cage and leave it in his backyard at his home on Lumpkin street, which was right across from where Georgia's practice football fields are located now.

And, every morning for the next two weeks, as I drove my bicycle to my job at the tennis courts, I would drive by Herschel's house and go into his backyard to see if our snakes had fought. But still, there they sat. Then one day I was startled—and pleased—to see that my king snake was all by himself in the cage. He also looked rather fat and seemed to have a smile on his face.

"ONWARD CHRISTIAN BULLDOGS"

(Following are two "prayers" offered by Magill at the annual Jacksonville Georgia Bulldog Club breakfast on the morning before the Georgia-Florida game.)

Lord, your Georgia Bulldog People are hunkered down on the banks of the St. John's here in Jacksonville on the morn of the ninth battle of the campaign of 1980.

In case you've overlooked it, Lord, we've won all the other battles, and please don't think us greedy in wanting to win them all. We covet only what every school covets: the national collegiate football championship! You let us come close to it in 1927, 1942, 1946 and 1971. You may not remember it but we do.

Lord, we wish to call your attention to a couple of facts. Your devoted disciple, St. Vincent the Merciful, has never had us on NCAA probation. He has been a good boy. He has sacrificed part of his hair. He has even sacrificed his wife Barbara's spleen to our noble cause, and I believe he would sacrifice even more— perhaps *her* hair—if need be.

Lord, we know you move in mysterious ways. We know that

after Coach Dooley banged his head against the windshield in his car wreck that our offensive strategy greatly improved the very next game.

Lord, we pray that you don't let these Florida Philistines do unto us today what we have done unto them so many times. Let us "do it unto them" just one more time.

Lord, you have stripped us of the Presidency when you won a "big one" for The Gipper. Now your Georgia Bulldog People have a Dream—a Dream of being No. 1 in the land.

We want you with us today as you were last week in the fourth quarter when you gave Scott Woerner the strength to smite loose the ball and Tim Parks the vision to find it.

Oh Lord, let our Dream come true. Free our people. Let "No. 1" ring throughout our land. From Ludowici westward to Tallapoosa . . . from Hiawasee down to Hahira, let No. 1 Ring! And, Lord, if you let all these good things come to pass, we promise to be as humble as Herschel.

AMEN

"ONWARD CHRISTIAN BULLDOGS," PART II

We've beaten Florida so many times it's hard to pick the game I like best.

Take the very first game in 1904. We won it, 52 to 0. Florida doesn't count it—typically. They claim that the Florida team we beat in 1904 was the University of Florida at Ocala. That's true, but a few years later they moved to Gainesville, and we can't help it that they were run out of Ocala.

There was something I liked about the 1942 game. I guess it was the score—75-0—run up by Sinkwich, Trippi and Company—the SEC and Rose Bowl Champions.

The sweetest victories, of course, are those in which you rally to win and snatch the candy out of the Gators' *big* mouths. Like 1975 when Richard Appleby faked the end-around and passed to Gene Washington, and the great 1976 comeback—down 27-13 at the half; final score, Georgia 41, Florida 27.

Like 1978 when we kept the ball the last seven minutes of the game to preserve a 24-22 victory. Like 1980 when Buck Belue passed to Lindsay Scott en route to the national championship. Like 1981 when Herschel Walker led a 95-yard drive against the clock, and like 1982 when a 99-yard drive in the fourth quarter won 10-9.

But I tell you what is going to be the sweetest Georgia victory ever, and that is the one the Big Red Team is going to chalk up today, November 9, 1985, when the No. 1 Gators get their royal come-uppance.

I have a *feeling* that it's going to be business as usual for the Georgia Bulldogs in the Gator Bowl today. Five years ago I stood before you at this great annual gathering of Red and Black loyalists and I gave a prayer that was answered with that immortal and monumental miracle—Buck Belue to Lindsay Scott.

My fellow Georgia Bulldogs, it's that time again. May we bow our heads!

Oh, Lord, your chosen people—the Georgia Bulldogs—are hunkered down on the Banks of the St. Johns in Jacksonville today. There are Bulldog tribes here from all over the land of Georgia—from Ludowici westward to Tallapoosa, from the mountains of Hiawassee downhill to Hahira.

They are here, Lord, to do battle with the Philistines of Florida—the best team that money can buy. We need your help. We know that you move in mysterious ways, Lord, but we don't understand how you could let so many of our fine boys get so banged up and yet you saved that good for nothing Bulldog, Lewis Grizzard.

I hope you're not inconvenienced, Lord, by the game not being on television today. But it ain't our fault. These Florida Philistines have broken more commandments than Moses ever dreamed of.

Lord, we admit that we are not completely without sin ourselves. Why, our own Kenny Sims has back-slid a little, and had to sit out the big Tulane game, but Brother Dooley in his infinite wisdom has decided that Kenny has repented enough to play today. And, we do need him today, Lord, and all the *other* help we can get, too.

Be with us today, Lord, and when you hear our Red Coat band playing, "Onward Christian Bulldogs," please shed thy grace on us. And, it needn't be a lop-sided win. Just one point will be fine, Oh, Lord.

AMEN

(Note: Georgia upset the No. 1 ranked Gators, 24-3, a few hours after that prayer.)

MAGILL WINS NATIONAL SPEED-TYPING TITLE

In 1946, the year after World War II had ended and I had been discharged from the United States Marine Corps, I laid proud claim to the national speed-typing championship.

I guess I was a prodigy because I began typing when I was two years old. My daddy had a typewriter at home, and I would practice on it, pretty much like Paderewski did on the piano at the same age, I suppose.

I remember as a boy, while writing high school sports at the *Athens Banner-Herald*, that the older writers often would stop their work just to marvel at my typing prowess. I still recall one of those smart alecks, whom I overheard saying: "That boy can't write a lick but he sho' can type. God moves in mysterious ways."

In the summer of 1946, while working on the *Atlanta Journal*, they held a special typing contest and the winner's score was entered in the national newspapermen's speed typing championships. How I coveted that title! So I oiled up my old L. C. Smith typewriter and could really make it hum. First, the *Journal* had to determine its champion, and they held departmental preliminary tournaments (society, advertising, circulation, business, editorial, newsroom, sports, etc.). I didn't see any reason to hold a sports department contest. There was no doubt that I was the best, but one day Ed Miles, a senior member of the sports staff, overheard me saying that I expected to represent the sports department in the upcoming championships and Miles immediately set me straight. He said to me: "Magill, you ain't going to represent the sports department; Mr. Danforth (the veteran sports editor) can type rings around you. He always represents us. But if you think you're better, you'll have to challenge him."

"Challenge him?" I stammered. I was already scared to death of Mr. Danforth and I wasn't about to challenge him at anything.

Then Miles egged me on, saying: "On second thought, I think you should challenge him. This matter needs to be settled once and for all. If you're afraid to go in his office and challenge him, just write him a letter. He can't do any worse than fire you."

I debated the rest of the day what to do. Miles kept egging me on with things like, "Are you a man or a mouse?"

I ended up by writing this letter: "Dear Mr. Danforth, Please do not consider this letter in any way an affront to your unquestioned leadership in our sports department. But can I challenge you for the right to represent the sports department in the *Journal* speed typing contest? Respectfully submitted, (signed) Daniel Hamilton Magill, Jr., Captain, USMCR

I must confess that I didn't walk into Mr. Danforth's office, slap his face and hand him my challenge. I waited till he had left the office, then slipped my letter onto his desk and backed out of the office, covering my tracks.

The next day, when he came to work, he picked up my letter, read it and stormed out of his office and came right up to where I was sitting. With a flourish in front of all, he ripped my letter to smithereens and spat out: "Today—at high noon."

Word spread like wildfire and it seemed as though everyone in the *Journal* building was there for the showdown at noon. The *Journal's* venerable and world-famous golf writer and incomparable raconteur, O. B. Keeler was in charge of the duel. With much ado, he called Mr. Danforth and me together in the middle of the room and went over the rules, which were: the contestants would type the same line, "Now is the time for all good men to come to the aid of their party," as many times as possible during a two minutes' time span. The typist with the most correct words would win. Mr. Danforth then went to his typewriter in his private, glass-enclosed office. I sat down at my desk. Then Mr. Keeler in a staccato voice yelled: "Typists ready. Take your marks." Bang! He fired a pistol—right into my ear, it seemed like, which caused me to get off to a bad start.

Nevertheless, I recovered and began banging away myself. I was sure I was winning because listening to his carriage bell told me I was typing two lines for every one of his. The contest ended with Mr. Keeler again firing his pistol which again seemed to explode in my ear. The next thing I knew, Ed Miles had come over and ripped out my page of typed lines, then he went to Mr. Danforth's office, whereupon Mr. Danforth handed him his page. Then Mr. Keeler and Miles compared the two pages. I fully expected Miles to announce that I had won, and I had already prepared a modest victory speech, giving much credit to Mr. Danforth, from whom I learned everything I knew, etc. But Miles announced in a loud voice: "The winner and still champion, Col. Edward Danforth."

I was flabbergasted, crestfallen. I went over to look at the two pages and saw that Mr. Danforth actually had five more lines than I did. I knew he couldn't have beaten me fair and square, but I certainly wasn't going to demand a recount or another match.

Well, the next day was to be the official *Journal* intra-departmental typing championships. Even though I was feeling low, I planned to go out and watch Mr. Danforth and pull for him to win. But a few minutes before the contest was to begin, Ed Miles came up to me and said, "I have just talked to Mr. Danforth, and he is sick. He wants you to take his place and represent the sports department."

Then Mr. Keeler called me aside and said: "Dan, don't you ever let out that I told you this, but Danforth cheated you yesterday. He already had a full page of lines typed before your contest started. Now, we want you to go out there and carry our flag high. You're the best we've ever had. Go out there and knock 'em dead."

Boy, was I now pumped up! I went out there and set my own personal record: 148 words a minute, and it won the national newspapermen's speed typing title for the *Atlanta Journal* that summer of 1946. I only used two fingers: my left index finger and my right forefinger.

MAGILL'S MONIKERS

As a boy sportswriter for my father's paper, the *Athens Banner-Herald*, I was indelibly impressed by the nicknames given almost all oustanding athletes: Ty Cobb was "the Georgia Peach"; Babe Ruth "the Sultan of Swat"; Jack Dempsey was named for his hometown, "the Manassa (Colorado) Mauler."

The *Atlanta Journal*'s Edwin Camp, who wrote under the pseudonym "Ole Timer," called Spurgeon Chandler "the Carnesville Ploughboy," a nickname Chandler proudly carried throughout his Georgia football career and with the world champion New York Yankees when he was baseball's MVP in 1943.

My father sent me to cover several big fights in New York City where I also was impressed by the inimitable ringside announcer, Harry Ballough, who always was quite alliterative in introducing the fighters. I will never forget his presentation of Joe Louis at his Billy Conn battle: ". . . the ebony embalmer, the deadly dynamiter from Detroit, boxing's celebrated, brilliant brown bomber . . ."

When I was prep editor of the *Atlanta Journal* right after World War II, I was excited about a fleet halfback from south Georgia, Lauren Hargrove, and I tagged him "the Fabulous Phantom of Fitzgerald." He went on to Georgia, and it was my pleasure as Georgia's sports information director to see him fully live up to that name against Auburn in Columbus in 1951. The Fabulous

The Fabulous Phantom of Fitzgerald

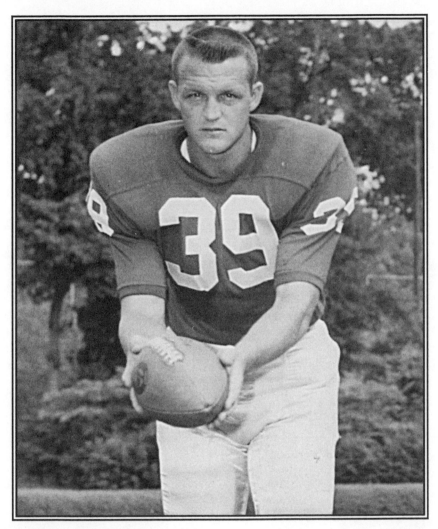

The Big Toe from Cairo

Phantom had a field day, including a 79-yard TD romp.

I can't remember the first nickname I gave a Georgia athlete, but it could have been "the Swamp Fox" for Francis Marion Campbell, All-America tackle at Georgia in the early 1950s, later all-pro with the world champion Philadelphia Eagles in 1960 and still later head coach for the Eagles and Atlanta Falcons. I simply gave him the nickname originally given South Carolina's revolu-

The Bootin' Teuton

tionary war hero, General Francis Marion, for whom Campbell, a native of Chester, South Carolina, undoubtedly was named.

Most of my names for Georgia football players were pretty corny: "the Chatham Cheetah," for a swift halfback from Savannah (county of Chatham), Julian Smiley; "the Gliding Ghost of Goodwater," for halfback Charley Harris of Goodwater, Alabama; quarterback Zeke Bratkowski, "the Pitching Pole"; fullback Theron Sapp, "Thundering Theron"; punter Bobby Walden, "the Big Toe from Cairo" (he hailed from Cairo, Georgia); punter Spike Jones, "Sputnik Spike" (he was kicking 'em a mile high when the Russian Sputnik originated); placekicker Peter Rajecki, a German, was "the Bootin' Teuton"; tail-

The Greek Streak

back Charley Trippi, "the Italian Stallion"; Herschel Walker, "the Goal-Line Stalker."

When I tagged halfback Jimmy Poulous "the Greek Streak," Georgia assistant coach Mike Castronis, a classmate of mine and

The Ebullient Embalmer

good friend, kidded me, "You never gave me a nickname when I made All-America." I retorted: "It's not too late. What about 'the Greek Freak' for you?"

I suppose the nickname I liked best was "the Ebullient Embalmer" for fullback Ronnie Jenkins, who always smiled after running over and knocking down his adversaries. Famed Dallas sports editor Blackie Sherrod noticed it in our brochure for the 1967 Cotton Bowl and complimented me on it.

REMEMBERING ROBERT WOODRUFF

I shall never forget the first time I met Mr. Robert Woodruff. It was back in those lazy, hazy summer days of the mid-1930s. I had caught the bus from Athens to Atlanta to play in the state junior tennis tournament, and the bus driver, whom I knew because I frequently rode his bus, made a special stop to let me out at the old Briarcliff Hotel on Ponce de Leon.

The Briarcliff then was a truly imposing hotel, being owned by Asa Candler, Jr., Coca-Cola's first mogul and Atlanta's wealthiest citizen at that time. Mr. Candler's wife, the former Helen Magill of Hartwell, was my great aunt, and it was no coincidence that the manager of the Briarcliff was her first cousin and my uncle, Jule Magill of Hartwell. It also was no coincidence that I was staying at the Briarcliff in a nice room at a special rate (free).

As I entered the main lobby of the hotel, a bellboy met me and grabbed my bag. I said to him, "Take me to the manager's office." He did, and when I greeted my uncle he introduced me to two other gentlemen who happened to be with him. One was the famous trainer of world champion boxers, Mike Cantrell, who had trained Max Baer, Jack Dempsey and Jim Jeffries, among many immortals of the ring. The other man was the new head of the Coca-Cola Company who was to eventually lead it to astronomical heights in the financial world, Robert W. Woodruff. Mr. Woodruff had a penthouse atop the Briarcliff where he had a gymnasium, and Mr. Cantrell had been employed as his trainer to keep him fit.

I recall Mr. Woodruff as a tall, handsome man who certainly

seemed fit, or "in the pink," as Mr. Cantrell would have wanted him to be. Mr. Cantrell spoke with an Irish brogue and must have come from the old country, as did so many of those prominent in the early days of boxing in the United States.

My uncle introduced me to these outstanding men, and he mentioned that Mr. Woodruff was "the head man of Coca-Cola." He introduced me as his nephew and also told Mr. Woodruff that my father was the editor of the *Athens Banner-Herald* and that I was the state table tennis champion. It was at this point that Mr. Woodruff and I had a "business" discussion. I told Mr. Woodruff that Coca-Cola was my favorite drink and that I even had a Coca-Cola drink stand at Georgia's tennis courts (the old clay courts by Woodruff Hall where the Journalism-Psychology building is now).

Mr. Woodruff asked me, "How have your sales been going?" I replied, "Very well, sir. We sold a full case last week."

"Are you keeping them good and cold?" Mr. Woodruff asked.

"Yes, sir," I replied. "I ride my bicycle to the ice house twice a day to make sure that our Coca-Colas are served 'ice cold.'"

"Excellent," he commented, and I believe that was about the extent of our "business" discussion that memorable day.

Today, as I look back on that episode, I wish I had had the presence of mind to have had my uncle, who could have been my "sports agent," get Mr. Woodruff to use my picture in a Coca-Cola advertisement saying, "State Ping Pong champion drinks Coca-Cola."

I bet it would have gotten more laughs than any of Rodney Dangerfield's TV commercials.

THE LONGEST POINT

The YMCAs of the United States pioneered in the promotion of quite a few sports. They invented basketball. That is, their James Naismith of the Springfield, Massachusetts, YMCA did, and I believe they also invented volleyball. I know for a fact that they first promoted softball, gymnastics, swimming, wrestling and table tennis in this country through their numerous YMCAs throughout the land.

The Athens YMCA is the third oldest "Y" in the U.S. and has had model programs from its very beginning. The University of Georgia's first basketball coach, the late Walter T. Forbes, was the physical director and general secretary of the Athens YMCA for many years. He was especially fond of ping pong, which is what table tennis was called when I was a boy.

"W.T." taught me how to play ping pong when I was eight years old, and I was 12 in 1933 when I stunned the local ping pong world by upsetting the state YMCA men's champion, Aaron Cohn of Columbus, in the Athens Y City tournament. Aaron was a student at UGA at the time, and he later was Georgia's tennis captain and now is a distinguished judge in his hometown.

My victory greatly pleased W.T., who considered me his "protege" and also said that I was a "prodigy," two words I had never previously heard and had no idea what meant. W.T. encouraged me to play in the State YMCA table tennis championships that were held each summer, rotating from one city to another. So I ventured forth and eventually won the State Y title 10 of 12 times during a 25 year period (1933 through 1958).

But this story is about the State YMCA tournament that happened to be held on my home table in Athens in 1936 when I played my fellow townsman and sparring partner, Vernon Boatner, in the finals. I was 15 and Vernon was 16. He later was a football star at old Athens High, having moved to Athens from Valdosta. (Incidentally, he was related to Valdosta's Buck Belue, the great quarterback on Georgia's 1980 national championship team, and one could easily tell they were related because they had the same kind of curly hair.)

Vernon and I played a lot in practice, and he raised his game to my level. We were both defensive players and had played several unusually long matches in Athens City tournaments, some points lasting over 30 minutes. For that reason, the referee (and timekeeper) of our state finals match, Dr. Milton. P. (Big Mit) Jarnagin, suggested we play only one game for the championship. We readily agreed.

I was leading, 3-2, when we played The Long Point—which is said to have been the longest point ever played. It lasted one hour and fifty-eight minutes.

Vernon won the celebrated point by hitting the edge of the table (the very end of the table on my side). I actually got my paddle on the ball and returned it, but the ball hit the top of the net and fell back on my side of the table, which so infuriated me that I immediately picked up the ball and put it back in play before Vernon could rest on his laurels. We had several more long points (not that long, though), and I won most of them to run up a lead of 16-8, at which time he abandoned his usual steady game and threw caution to the wind, trying to slam every ball as hard as he could, and I won the game and the match, 21-9.

One more interesting note on this long point: When it began, one of the spectators, the late Ed Landau, Sr., of Albany (a Georgia student who roomed at the Y with future Athens National Bank president Tommy Milner), wandered in on the match and asked Dr. Jarnagin the score, to which Dr. Jarnigan replied, "3-2, Magill." Landau then went up town to take in a movie and when he returned after seeing the movie, he again asked Dr. Jarnagin the score. "3-2, Magill," replied Dr. Jarnagin. "That's what you told me before I went to the movie," said Landau. "That's what it still is," said Dr. Jarnigan.

I employed a most unorthodox grip on my paddle due to the fact that I could barely see above the table when I began playing at age eight, and I had to hit up on every ball. And I hit every shot (forehand and backhand) on the same side of the paddle. After growing up, I still used my peculiar style of hitting the ball on the same side on the paddle, and in 1982 when I went to Beijing to teach tennis to the Chinese professionals, I watched the Chinese world champion table tennis players practice, and I was delighted to see that they also hit the ball on the same side of the paddle on each shot—except they used a different grip, the famous pen-holder grip.

The most fame I ever received from my ping pong days, though, was through Coach Wallace Butts. I'd introduce Coach Butts at various Bulldog Club meetings throughout the state, bragging on him quite a bit, following which Coach Butts (thinking he ought to say something good about me) would say with a big smile: "You know, Dan used to be state ping pong champion—and I understand he was very good at tiddlywinks too." I do believe Coach Butts got about as big a kick out of those remarks as anything he ever said at our Bulldog meetings.

UGA, Mascot for the Ages

All athletic teams have nicknames or mascots or both. Georgia had a mascot for its first football game against Auburn in 1892: A billygoat adorned in a black coat with red "U.G." letters on each side. Two years later the Georgia mascot was a solid white bull terrier owned by a student, the late Charles Black, Sr., of

UGA I with cheerleader Hannah Jones

Atlanta, whose family had many distinguished Georgia alumni.

In the early 1920s Georgia's football team acquired the nickname "Bulldogs" because an Atlanta sportswriter described their play as "tenacious as a bulldog." The name stuck, and from time to time various supporters have loaned their bulldogs to the team for certain games. The current dynasty of UGAs was begun by Georgia alumni Frank (Sonny) Seiler, now a member of the Georgia Athletic Board, and his wife, Cecelia, of Savannah. In fact, UGA I was the grandson of a former white English bulldog who traveled with the Bulldogs to the Rose Bowl in Pasadena New Year's Day, 1943. It was owned by Frank Heard of Columbus, and UGA I—originally named "Hood's Ole Dan"—was born in Columbus December 2, 1955. As a puppy, he was given to Cecelia Seiler, a native of Columbus.

I well remember how UGA I became Goergia's official mascot. From 1947 through 1955 Georgia's mascots were brindled English bulldogs: Butch, owned by Mabry Smith of Warner Robbins, Georgia, 1947-50; and Mike, owned by C. L. Fain of Atlanta, 1951-55. Mike lived in the old athletic fieldhouse (now the Alumni House), and when he died Coach Butts asked me to find a replacement. I had stories placed in the newspapers announcing that a search was underway to find a new mascot and that those interested should contact me. Immediately, a Georgia law school student, who was working in the athletic ticket office, came up to my sports information office, then located at Stegeman Hall. He was Sonny Seiler, whom I had first known when he was a member of the Georgia swimming team as an undergraduate student.

Sonny said he and his wife had a bulldog puppy whose grandfather was Georgia's mascot in the Rose Bowl. Sonny invited me to his apartment to see the puppy, and he looked good to me. I told Coach Butts that the Seilers had a fine young bulldog, and Coach Butts said, "Put him to work."

From that moment on I believe that Sonny and Cecelia Seiler have done the finest job in the history of raising mascots for athletic teams. Georgia's bulldog mascots are now the most famous in the country. They are the only mascots who are buried in the confines of their stadium. They are buried in cement vaults near the main gate in the embankment of the South stands with epitaphs inscribed in Georgia marble. These memorials attract hundreds of fans and visitors.

The Seilers named their first mascot UGA I (rhymes with mugger), and he served 11 years, being succeeded by his son, UGA II, at an impressive pregame ceremony at Homecoming, 1966. With the Georgia Redcoat Band lining the field, UGA II was led to the center of the field by Charles Seiler, son of Sonny and Cecelia. The student body erupted in a cheer that was picked up by the entire stadium: "Damn Good Dog."

UGA II had an impressive reign as he watched Georgia participate in five bowl games and win two SEC championships. He died in 1972 and was succeeded by UGA III, who led Georgia to six bowl games and closed out his career magnificently at the Sugar Bowl New Year's Day, 1981, as Georgia won the national championship.

UGA IV attended a bowl game every year of his reign, 1984-89.

UGA V was born March 6, 1990, and I am proud, indeed, that my longtime friends, Sonny and Cecelia Seiler, named him Magillicuddy, which caused a nurse at Athens Hospital to say to my son, a cardiologist there:

"Dr. Magill, I think it's just wonderful that the new Georgia bulldog mascot has been named for your father. What a fine honor!" To which my son replied, "Why, that's no big deal. I was named for him, too."

On Induction into Blue Key, 1983

I greatly appreciate this high honor accorded me but I must confess to you that I feel more ill at ease than usual tonight. The reason is that Tyus Butler was my major professor when I was a student at Henry W. Grady School of Journalism, and I am sure that at this moment he must think he is dreaming when he sees me up here on this pedestal.

I really believe I could have succeeded in my journalism work under Professor Butler had not the Bulldog Duckpin Bowling Alleys been located right across the street from the main campus. I spent a great deal of my college life there playing the most fascinating sport I have ever known: Odd-Pins. In this game, you and your partner take turns knocking down the pins, and you attempt to knock down an odd number—an even number is scored as zero.

While Tyus was no doubt disgusted with my efforts in his classes, I feel that he must have been somehow proud of me when I won the University duckpin bowling title twice; and five years after my graduation—in 1947 at Norfolk, Virginia, I had the high honor of being the lead-off man for the Atlanta All-Stars in the World Duckpin Team championship finals. I only mention this because none of the write-ups on me this week said a word about this honor.

I also would like to mention that in our group of odd-pin players, three of them—all University of Georgia alumni—really amounted to something of note. One was big Hugh O'Farrell, former Georgia football end whose father was a famous Athens marshal. Hugh in those days was known as Fireball O'Farrell, and later as Lt. Col. O'Farrell when he was one of World War II's most decorated heroes as a tank commander for George Patton. The tactics Col. O'Farrell used in Europe were the same as those that he had employed in bowling. He aimed his tanks straight at the head pin, or rather the point of the enemy forces, and smashed them. And it was uncanny how he always seemed to destroy an *odd* number of German tanks.

A second member of this group was one of my Sunday school classmates as a boy, Alvin Brackett, who became one of the leading Baptist ministers in the state. I have often wondered, "What went wrong with Alvin?"

A third member, who served as our scorekeeper, referee and bookie, was Dr. Milton P. (Big Mit) Jarnagin, Jr., a Rhodes Scholar, later to become one of the most distinguished mathematicians in the world—Chief of the Computations Division of the U.S. Guided Missile Center, Chicateague, Virginia. It was his grave responsibility to see that our missiles hit their targets if we ever went to war with Russia.

And I myself have gone on to enjoy a lifetime of athletics at the University of Georgia.

Back in 1959, when we were just getting over an eight-year losing streak to Georgia Tech in football, I heard some wonderful words uttered by one of the greatest Georgia Bulldogs ever, William Chenault (Bill) Munday. We were playing The Enemy on Grant Field and had a good lead at halftime. Bill was interviewing me on the radio at halftime, and said: "You know, Dan, life can be truly glorious when you are leading Georgia Tech on Grant Field, 21-0, at halftime."

And that's the way it has been for me most of my time at the University of Georgia: truly glorious!

INDEX